ABOVE AND BEYOND
THE CALL OF DUTY
FOR *Love*

Above and Beyond
THE CALL OF DUTY
for Love

TJ Allen

To order additional copies of this book, contact:
Xlibris Corporation
1-888-795-4274
www.Xlibris.com
Orders@Xlibris.com
127611

Above and Beyond the call of duty all for love

For the love of our great country, men and women join the Armed Forces in the continued fight to protect the people of the United States of America.

Military recruiters get your everyday volunteer to sign a contract of Defense and promise to assist in fulfilling each person's ambition to be trained as an engineer, pilot, doctor, lawyer, police officer, nurse, electronics technicians, computer analysis, air traffic controllers, ECT. A career with the Military offers job opportunities and education at no cost other than serving your country for 4, 6, 8, 10 years and more if those persons wish to retire. Once enrolled and accepted, you belong to a Government Family that will come first. Any other family is secondary. Once in, each recruits life is changed forever. That person who you knew prior to signing the contract is now a soldier, fighter, killing machine if necessary before beginning any career goals. Feelings will be lost within oneself due to the combat training each experience.

Once each makes it through boot camp and graduates and receives their first set of orders, an emotional rollercoaster begins. The soldiers who had ridged discipline as pre teens and teens adjust better to taking orders everyday and those who had liberal upbringings.

The brainwashing of country first can be seen and felt by the soldiers' mates and spouses. It is quite noticeable. Your tender, loving partner is not that into companionship anymore. If their partners wait it out, it will slowly return.

For me, I noticed on day one of my partners return. However, two months later and several letters asking me to join him in his contractual adventure. I agreed, however, there was one catch. We had to be married. That was the only way I could be with him and support him through his six year contact with the Military.

I did try to get him to believe that I would wait the six years for him but the Military's brainwashing told him that "most of you will receive "Dear John" letters ending the relationships you once had." Funny. I didn't even know what a "Dear John" letter was until he told me.

Between the phone calls and the loneliness emotions expressed in his letters, I agreed to marry him.

We were married on Valentine's Day. Two months later we were off to his first assigned destination. We were both young and about to find out the hard way what the Military meaning of "If we had wanted you to have a family we would have issued you one".

Uncle Sam was the number one priority and not anything else. It's too bad that things fell into place the way they fell for a lot of partners. It's a good thing that nightmares go away when we awake. However, this dream was everlasting.

Chapter 1

I received a phone call from an attorney by the name of Lee Waters. He explained, in Hawaii he was defending two acquaintances of mine named Joseph and Kelly Chambers. He further said that he needed a character witness on their behalves.

Interested, I asked, "What does this case pertain to?"

He said he would only reveal that information if I agreed to be flown to Hawaii to be such a witness.

I laughed over the phone and thought to myself, this attorney isn't dumb. Then I replied, "If all expenses are paid I would gladly come and testify for the two of them."

He responded, "Yes all expenses paid including time missed from your employment.

I made the comment, "My testimony must really be a necessity considering the expenses involved in bringing me out there".

He replied, "It's not just important, it is probably our last hope of winning this case."

Surprised at his response, I said, "That's a pretty negative attitude, Sir. Will you tell me about this long shot case so I could prepare myself, please? By the way, for us not to have too radical of a cross examination of my testimony use my maiden name on the witness sheet. That way the Prosecutor will have less time to prepare a rebuttal. Now, you were going to reply."

He replied, "Your last thought is well taken and quite good. Now about the case: the Military wants to keep the Defendants' in the Armed Forces until their terms are completed. However, upon completion of their terms, they would not have a marriage due to the stress which Military life tends to bring upon couples."

I said to Lee, "asking me to be a witness is a good idea; plus, if we 'play our cards right' and I can win the sympathy of the council, your negative outlook of this case could turn into a win against the Military. Come to think of it, I don't know that much about their marriage but if we mix my Divorce in with the possibility of theirs, we could find ourselves standing on pretty firm ground. When do I leave?"

Lee said, "You leave tomorrow and your strategy is on target. You are to depart at 7:00 a.m. on American Airlines flight 523."

I remarked, "You knew I would accept the challenge before talking to me."

Lee said, "See you in Hawaii."

Before Lee hung-up the phone I commented, "I hope the rewards are sweat."

I could hear Lee laughing as he hung the phone up.

After the phone call, I made arrangements to be absent from work for at least a week. My boss gave me 8 days off and asked me to call if there was going to be a delay. I told him fine and thanks.

I spent the rest of the day packing for the journey and thinking about how much I knew of Joe and Linda's marriage. It wasn't much but mixing the fact that I am Divorced from a Marine just might be enough. Reminiscing: Linda and I did have some fun times before my ex-husband and I went our separate ways. We had worked together in the Exchange and we got to know about each other's marital problems.

Bouncing back to reality, I was hoping that Linda and Joe had not told my ex-husband I was going to be their witness. We haven't seen each other in over two years, He still means a lot to me, but we became two different units going in opposite directions for a married couple.

After packing and double checking to make sure I had everything, I thought of the possible questions that the Defense Attorney and the Prosecuting Attorney would ask. It could get pretty dirty. Oh well, I feel really confident about the subject-matter and my experiences while married to a Marine.

One thing's for certain, Military life is not like the real-world.

It was getting late so I sat the alarm for 4:30 a.m. and turned in for the night.

Chapter 2

Morning came quickly. I showered, dressed and put everything into the car. Onward to the airport I drove. I parked my auto and proceeded to the Reservation's Desk. I told the clerk my name and she gave me a ticket for First Class.

Smiling I thought to me, a lot of money is being spent on this case. I hope my testimony proves to be worth the expense. I never thought being a Military divorcee would be of value; however, Attorney Lee Waters seems to think it's of great value. I must be the key that screws the Military. We shall see how well the key fits.

On the plane I decided that I was just going to relax. After-all, why get anxious over an event that is 12 hours away. I had the pleasure of sitting next to a businessman from Texas. We had a delightful conversation and it was too bad I could not layover in L.A. for we could have had some fun.

Thinking of that, I wondered how long this case would last. I could only mentally hold out sexually for a week before Depression set in. However, if we win the case, I was going to get a sweat reward from a smooth-talking attorney. Nothing in this world is free.

In L.A. the flight had a short lay-over. I bid farewell to my Texas businessman and told him maybe we would meet again.

Re-boarding the plane, I was on my way to Hawaii. I did not have anyone seated beside me. It was a rather boring end to a long trip.

When Lee and I talked on the phone, he didn't mention who was picking me up at the airport. I always hated seeing chauffeurs standing at the gate with signs displaying people's names on them. Now, my name just might be on-one of those signs.

At that point I began feeling the anticipation. I was really hoping not to see my ex-husband at all while in Hawaii. Our marriage did not end on very pleasant terms. The last time he was home he refused to see me. I guess he could not put with the Military gossip. One day he'll accept the past for what it was.

"Fasten seat belts. We will be landing shortly," said the Captain. Here already! On the ground at the airport, I felt a lot of old memories stirring inside of me. Oh well, now is now and then was then. I was a different person today and I was getting a chance to show it. The worst part, I knew that in the courtroom all the old wounds were going to be reopened.

Entering the lobby, sure enough there was a man holding a sign with my name printed on it. I began to laugh to myself; I approached him and said hello acknowledging that I was the person he was waiting for.

He said, "I'm Charles, Lee's assistant. As we walked to baggage claim, he asked, "How was your flight?"

I said, Long and tiring. How is the case so far?"

Picking up my baggage he said, "In my opinion not good. Most of the witnesses for our case were not able to shed much light on the subject-matter. As you may know we are trying to prove that the longer the Defendants' stay in the Military the worst their marriage will be and thus result in divorce."

I asked, "Well, what is the Prosecutor's response?"

He replied, "They claim that counseling is available to help with the marital problem. Furthermore, the two signed a contract and should have to up-hold the terms."

I made the comment, "It's all for the Military and nothing for humanity."

Understanding my quote Charles said, "You said it. Not to make you nervous but all the other witnesses for our case have been discredited. You are our last hope."

As we headed for the car I pondered over what he had said.

In the car I asked, "How thorough of an investigation did you on me?"

He said, "I don't know what you mean?"

I said, in order for me to be the deciding factor in this case your investigation had to have been pretty thorough."

He commented, "We know only what Linda and Joe knew. Your ex-husband wanted no part in the case since he is leaving the island soon."

I commented, "That sounds like him."

Further he said, "You tell what you want to tell. Remember, you're under oath and hopefully all that you tell will help our case.

However, we feel that none of your testimony will be discredited because you're bright."

I said, "Correction! Not because I'm bright, but because I have a back-ground in Law?"

Charles began to laugh. At the Hyatt Hotel, we checked me in to room 126. Charles tipped the bell-hop for carrying my baggage to the room.

Charles said, "I'll telephone Lee and find out when you are scheduled to appear for testimony."

While Charles spoke with Lee on the phone, I admired the view of Hawaii from the window. It sure did bring back memories. Then I looked around the room. It was nothing spectacular.

Charles hung the phone up and said, "You are to be called to testify in the morning, 10:00 a.m. Do you want to go out to dinner or eat here?"

At that point I was getting a little irritated with the 'attorney-client' routine of his voice. I turned to answer his question.

I answered, "We can go out, but only if you act yourself not like you're on stage giving a performance."

I could see he was somewhat set-back by my words, but I didn't care to explain.

He thought to himself for a few moments and finally said, "How's the Seafood House sound?"

I laughed and said, "Okay". Let me freshen up a little."

Out of the blue, Charles made the comment, "you don't use make-up?"

I replied, "That's right. I am a southern girl and believe that nature is the best make-up. Why cover-up what the good Lord gave me?"

He sighed and said, "That's the type of answers we want tomorrow. Let's go."

On the way to dinner I asked, "Are you married?"

He said, "No. But I do have a steady girl-friend."

I said, "That's nice."

We walked into the restaurant. Apparently, he had made reservations in advance.

I looked at him and said, "So far someone's fed you all the right information."

Charles just laughed. The waitress took our order. Lobster for Charles; Crab-legs for me. Then my suspicions surfaced.

I looked at Charles and said, "Well let's see: $700 airfare, $60 a night room, $75 a day for meals. That's a lot of money.

Therefore, money must be involved in this case, too. So what's this case completely about?"

Charles did not quite understand the question. So I put it another way.

I said, "This case is obviously about the marriage of the Defendants'. However, Mr. Waters is not spending all this money to just win a case against the Military. Is there movie rights involved, maybe book rights, or maybe a pretty penny?"

Charles sipped on his matinee and said, "Lee thought you would ask that question. Well, it involves $30,000 that the Military paid to the Defendants' for their service.

I said, "I have seen couples have to pay back money to the government for not fulfilling their contracts."

Charles said, "The two have put in all but one year, and the state of their marriage shows it, too."

I said, "Therefore, you would like to see the two start again with a year's bonus pay."

Charles said, "Lee and I think they deserve it."

Out of the ordinary I asked, "What if you lose?"

Charles was caught off guard again. From the look on his face I could tell he hadn't given the negative out-come much thought after viewing my past.

I interrupted his train of thought, "I realize you and Lee don't lose anything, but how about your clients?"

Charles finally answered, "The money and each other."

With that I changed the subject as our dinner arrived.

I asked, "Is your partner a good attorney?"

He replied, "One of Hawaii's finest."

I asked, "Is he married or single?"

Charles said, "Married with 2 kids, a boy and a girl."

I then smiled and said, "Enjoy your meal. We have a long day to look forward to tomorrow.

Dinner was good. Charles and I conversed with small talk through dinner. I felt enough had been said about the case. The waitress brought the check. Charles left a tip on the table and paid on our way out. We drove silently back to the Hotel.

I'd rather walk into the courtroom knowing what is to be accomplished."

Charles said, "Lee said you would ask for all the information."

I said, "I'm looking forward to meeting Lee. Good-night Charles."

Charles replied, "Good-night. Pick you up at 8:00 a.m."

Back in my room I took off my clothes. I looked in the mirror and said to myself, give'm hell tomorrow kid. Then I was feeling rather aroused thinking that this case was riding on me. I decided to take a cold shower and then a warm one. As the cold water ran over my body, I became more and more aroused. So I began to masturbate the feelings away. Slowly massaging my clit, I inched my fingers inside of me. With the use of the cold water and my fingers stimulating the walls of my vagina, I experienced a small but necessary orgasm. After my clit was partially satisfied, I turned the water nozzle to warm. After the shower, I dried off with a soft towel and slipped my naked body into bed and fell asleep.

Chapter 3

Morning came too soon as I awoke from a dreamy sleep about the sexual reward I desired from an attorney I had not met yet. I arose from the bed, flushed my face with water and dressed comfortably in a leisure suit. I thought to myself how I always hated when someone tried to discredit me on anything. I told myself just to have patience and take it slow. After dressing, there was a knock at the door. I answered. There was a man standing there whom I did not know.

He smiled and said, "hi Tina. I'm Lee Waters. Charles is running a little late, but he's on his way."

As I admired his 6'2, 180 lb., dark hair and skin to match, plus mustache, I said, "pleasure to meet you; Come, in. I was just finishing getting ready. You are a pretty good looking attorney, with two kids."

Lee smiled and said, "Thank you. Are you nervous?"

I answered, "a little."

He asked, "Do you have any questions?"

I said, "Just one. If we win, which I think we shall, do I get a bonus?"

Lee laughed and replied, "first things first. We have to win."

I don't know if he actually understood my suggestiveness or not. But if Linda told him anything about my sexual habits then he had to have understood. A knock came at the door. Lee opened it.

Charles came in and asked, "Are you ready to go?"

I gathered my things together and said, "Let's give'm hell."

We all laughed as we left the room.

Charles said, "Over breakfast Lee and I will discuss with you what we hope to gain from your testimony that other witnesses could not provide."

I said, "Breakfast it is then."

On the way to breakfast I thought to myself what more could be said that hasn't already been said. I know I have to win the sympathy of the council. That should not be too hard; on the other hand, if this board is pro-military as in the early days it could be quite difficult.

We arrived at the restaurant and ordered.

Lee said, "Tina I know you don't know a whole lot about the Chamber's marriage; however, it's not as much what you know as how well you can tie your own experiences in with theirs."

As a wise-crack I made the comment, "So it's more like I am on trial not necessarily them and I have to re-live all of my nightmares."

Lee said bluntly, "That's right. Treat this case like it is your own, but remember **that** is the Chamber's case."

I asked, "What happened with the rest of your witnesses?"

Lee replied, "They were all married and had not experienced a divorce over military issues like you. Most of their testimony was more conclusive rather than factual, therefore the Prosecutor objected and the Chairman threw it out."

I asked, "That's why I am the last hope this case has of success?"

I smiled with confidence and stated, "Be ready to produce my bonus."

Charles gave me a puzzled look and Lee just smiled. Breakfast arrived at that moment. From then on Charles and Lee discussed their strategy for the case while we ate. I thought to myself, yes it's definitely going to be a long day. After breakfast, we drove to the courthouse. I could feel the butterflies swimming in my stomach. Once at the courthouse I began to relax.

I was seated in the waiting room till I was called.

Lee said, "Well, I'll see you in about 10 minutes."

I said, "I'll be there."

Charles smiled and said, "With that confident look on your face we might just win."

A Military Police Officer stayed in the room with me. He turned a voice monitor on. I could hear the sound of a crowd. Then the words

"This court will now come to order." You may be all seated." "Defense, call your witness."

Lee said, "I call Ms. Tina Williams to the stand."

I was escorted in by the Officer. I approached the stand. The Officer said, as he held a Bible in his hand, "Do you swear to tell the whole truth and nothing but the truth?"

I said, "I do."

He said, "You may be seated."

Lee stood from his seat and walked over to me. I couldn't help but to take notice of his gait and body in the nice-fitting beige suit. At that point I was relaxed. I quickly erase my mind of the passion and began to concentrate fully on the questions Lee was going to ask of me.

Standing in front of me Lee said Ms. Williams will you please tell the court your name prior to today."

I replied, "Mrs. Tina Allen."

Lee continued, "How do you know the Defendants?"

I replied, "Through my ex-husband."

Lee asked, "Is your ex-husband a member of the Service?"

I answered, "Yes."

Lee said, "Will you please tell the court your ex-husband's Name, Rank, and Work section."

I said, "Timothy Scott Allen, Corporal, assigned to USMC's Air-traffic Control unit."

Lee asked, "Is that how you came to know the Defendants?"

I answered, "Yes, through my ex-husband".

Lee said, "Ms. Williams will you please tell the court howl: you came to know the Chamber's from the beginning to now."

I was surprised to see that the Prosecutor was going to allow me to voice that knowledge but he did not object.

I answered, "I know that the two met in North Carolina and were married prior to honoring orders to Hawaii."

Lee interrupted, "You did not know the Defendants before Hawaii?"

I replied, "That's correct. My marriage at that time was on the verge of breaking apart. Therefore, my ex-husband and I did not socialize with too many people, including the people he worked with."

Lee said, "Continue with your recount of the Chambers."

I continued, "Here in Hawaii we met at a company party. Linda Chambers and I worked together at the Exchange. She was placed at the Exchange on duty as an Identification checker for a months' time. I was a Security Guard for the Exchange. Thus, we worked together."

Lee asked, "Did the two of you talk together?"

I said, "Yes".

Lee asked, "Did the conversations deal only with business?"

I replied, "No. We talked about our personal problems, too. She knew mine and I knew hers."

Lee asked, "Was the Marine Corps a problem for the two of them?"

I said, "Not the Marine Corps as a whole."

Lee asked, "What do you mean?"

I said, "Well, the Marine Corps as a whole quite understood to both parties. They both believed in fighting for the same cause. There was not a misunderstanding about defending one's country."

Lee asked, "Did the defendant ever say what her problems were?"

I answered, "Yes. The main problem was that they both were Air-traffic Controllers."

Lee said, "So we have two people with the same job function which is producing a problem."

I said, "Well, you have to understand that some couples with the same career goals understand each other and get along fine.

Then, you have couples like my ex-husband and I who have different career goals and don't get along well at all since they are venturing into conflicting goals. As for the Defendants, you have a couple who are both engaged in a highly stressful position where each has hundreds of lives in his hands and one wrong call could mean disaster."

Lee said, "There are other positions in the Military that can end in disaster, also."

I replied, "Yes, but they don't head the top 10 on the 'Most Stressful Job' list."

Prosecutor interrupted, "Objection. That is a statistical reference not entered into evidence. It's a conclusion by the witness."

Before the Chairman could answer sustained:

I said, "No sir. I am living proof of how stressful the job can be on a wife of an Air-traffic Controller."

Mr. Chairman said, "Sustained. Ms. Williams please do not use statistical data in your testimony. Since it is almost noon, we will resume testimony after lunch at 1400 hours."

Charles, Lee and I left the courtroom together for lunch.

During lunch I asked, "Why isn't the Prosecutor objecting to your line of questioning and my answers?"

Tee said, "Because he mainly waits to discredit my witnesses through cross examination. Plus, this is a civil matter rather than a criminal matter. What we are after is to get Joseph and Linda out of the Corps a year and a half early and not to repay the bonus money."

I asked, "They have to repay all the money or just a portion?"

Lee said, "According to the Corps, all the money for not fulfilling the contract."

I said, "So it's them out and the money, too. This might be tougher than we thought."

Lee said, "Well, you have made some points with the council, and we haven't really begun to explore Linda and Joseph's marriage. So really, we look pretty good. You aren't going to get hammered by the prosecution today. I intend to take my time on the problems of the marriage."

I said, "Well councilor, it's your ball-game."

Lee said, "Yes, and you're the winning run."

I amusingly said, "I like the excitement of being the home-run for the case."

Back in the courtroom, I re-took the stand and was reminded that I was still under oath.

Lee approached the stand and asked, "Ms. Williams will you please continue your story in Hawaii at the exchange?"

I said, "As I was saying before, Air-traffic controllers have a lot of people's lives in their hands. When two people are married and have the same Position, they tend to take work home with them. One person's stress can bring on another's especially when the two know each other's job. Well, this was a problem within their marriage. One handling a situation positively; the other, given the same situation, blows it."

Lee interrupted, "So Ms. Williams, what you are saying is that the stress from their job caused their marital problems?"

I answered, "The Marine Corps does give people examples and opportunity to take their stress out physically. However, in a stressful position, no one stops to think of the mental strain that air-traffic control provides. Therefore, yes, job stress can and does lead to marital stress. As in my own marriage, job stress was handled physically with outside activities. Well, too many outside activities to handle job stress are substituting the problem. Now you have one parties mind off stress, but that person is away from home causing the other party to wonder. Thus, more problems occur. Stress needs to be attacked through communication."

Lee asked, "Ms. Williams was communication a problem in the Defendant's marriage?"

I answered, "Yes. Communication is a problem in many marriages within the Marine Corps."

Lee asked, "Ms. Williams, shouldn't their stress have been handled easily by communication since they both have the same job?"

I replied, "Through personal experience, people would rather handle their own stress especially when the same careers are involved. The competition is great even when you are married. Therefore, communication can be hampered."

Lee asked, "What you are saying is that job stress is the problem in their marriage as it was in your dissolved marriage?"

I said, "Yes, because one stressful task makes other easily performed marital relations difficult."

Lee asked, "Did the defendant, Mrs. Chambers, discuss any other problems with you?"

I replied, "The other problems can easily be traced back to the job stress problem."

Prosecution said, "Objection. Witness is giving a conclusion."

Council said, "Sustained. The conclusion will be stricken."

Lee said, "Please tell the court any other problems you discussed with the defendant."

I continued, "While the defendant Linda Chambers and I were working in the exchange, I explained that my husband and I were having sexual problems. She made the comment that she and Joseph also were having sexual problems. I made the comment that mine must be mentally related since I could get the physical reaction but he was too pre-occupied. Linda agreed with me."

Tee asked, "Any other problems that you can tell us about?"

I said, "Linda did mention that Joseph had problems relating to women since he was raised by mother."

Lee asked, "Then you knew that Joseph was an abused child?"

I said, "Yes, I knew."

Lee asked, "How did that affect their marriage?"

I replied, "Linda told me that that was a big problem. My husband carried our pasts forward 'til the end."

Lee asked, "Would the defendant's past be known by the Military?"

Prosecution said, "Objection. Witness has no proof of such technicalities."

Council said, "If the witness can show such proof I will allow the answer."

I said, "My knowledge of air traffic control tells me that the Military did know but overlooked it."

Prosecution said, "Objection. Without proper justification that statement is a discredit to the Military."

Council said, "Ms. Williams we need justification of those circumstances.

Therefore, either you show such or I shall have to throw out the answer."

Lee said, "I can assure that the witness can show such justification." Ms. Williams will you please tell the court how you can justify your statements."

Taken back somewhat, I said, "In Carolina I was sexually assaulted by another air traffic controller who worked with my husband. In order for my spouse to get out of the Marine Corps, he had to have a valid reason. My spouse told his supervisors that he could not work with the person who assaulted his wife. His supervisors requested a statement from me detailing the whole incident as I remembered it. I wrote as detailed a statement as I could, signed that statement and it was presented to the Military supervisors. No action was taken against the other controller or to release my spouse from the military as per requested. I was told by my spouse that my statement had been shredded. Nothing ever came of the issue again until my spouse was asked to accept orders to another station. The request was granted although we still had a contract to fill at the Carolina duty station."

Lee interrupted, "Do we understand correctly that the whole incident was overlooked?"

I replied, "The assault, request for release, and the extreme mental strain on our marriage were all overlooked and discarded."

Lee asked, "What is the application of the defendants?"

I replied, "In application to the defendants, the Military has covered The defendant's past from the very beginning and today has only contributed to the problem which is going to cost defendants if they are released from service, they will need to spend a lot of time talking with counselors. Together they must deal with Joseph's past, their job stress and problems in their marriage."

Lee asked, "The problems are going to persist even though they are released?"

I replied, "Yes. The past isn't going to be erased when they get out. Just like in my relationship and at present divorce, the past is still present and must be dealt with positively. Having the defendants stay in the military is only going to continue to cost the military valuable time and money in the future."

Lee asked, "Were you and your spouse counseled?"

I replied, "Yes, three months."

Lee asked, "But you are divorced?"

I replied, "We needed more counseling but the military intervened with its duties and we did not receive more. We had too little time for our own lives. Therefore, the stress of past and future military service was the key to our divorce."

Lee asked, "Continued military service could hamper the defendants lives?"

I replied, "Yes. With a divorce or without, both are still going to incur some problems on top of what they already are experiencing. They have mentally failed as military personnel. Why the military wants to keep a couple that could cost them plenty escapes me."

Lee said, "No further questions."

Lee turned to the Prosecution and said, "Your witness."

Prosecutor said, "Council it's almost five o'clock. I would like to request that we continue with my examination of this witness tomorrow morning."

The Chairman said, "Request is granted. Court will re-adjourn at ten am."

I couldn't wait to get out of the hot seat. I was tired and hungry. Charlie and Lee took me to dinner. On the way, I just sat back and relaxed my mind. I eventually brought myself to asks, "How does our case look now?"

Charlie replied, "Pretty damn good. As long as the prosecution does not eat us up. You supplied him with a lot to work with. So it is going to come down to how well you hold your composure tomorrow."

Lee nodded his head in agreement. Lee seamed deep in thought while Charlie was interpreting today's events. Once at the restaurant, I decided we should have a more relaxed evening instead of talking about the case. After all, it's the prosecution's case now.

I made the suggestion and Lee and Charlie agreed. So we had dinner and talked about family and what the future held.

After dinner, Tee and Charlie escorted me back to the hotel room. There was no mention of the case before calling it a night. Charlie and Lee left after I entered my room.

In my opinion, a lot had been said today and possibly more than Lee had anticipated. However, deep down I was very sure and positive of all that had been revealed today. So I decided just to relax. I took a shower, listened to the radio and fell asleep.

The next day, I awoke after a comfortable sleep. I got myself dressed and ready for this last day of testimony. It was "do or die" time.

Well, Lee and Charlie arrived at my room. I ordered room-service while they went over some last minute details. Breakfast arrived.

While we ate, lee told me a few facts about the Prosecutor. I said, "Just give me an idea of what type of personality I *AM* working against."

Lee commented, "Egotistical." I replied, "my type of mans"

Chapter 4

As we walked in to the courtroom I said, "Back to the courtroom."

Lee said, "I will try and prevent the prosecutor from bringing up too much about your past; after all you aren't on trial. However, you have given him a lot to work with."

I sat back and waited for the trial to begin. I thought of all of the sarcastic answers I could give in response to the questions of the prosecutor. I could just imagine all the 'mud' he was going to sling-around the courtroom. However, I told myself, "stand tall and firm on all I had opened myself up for."

It was time to stop day-dreaming of the events to come and start living them. "Please stand." The council members entered the courtroom. "Please be seated."

The chairman said, "Prosecution please continue with the cross-examination of the last witness."

Prosecutor asked, "May I please approach the bench with the defense council?"

The councilmen answered, "Permission granted."

Prosecutor asked, "May I have a recess until afternoon so I can properly prepare for cross-examination of the witness?"

The councilman said, "Permission granted. This court is in recess until 1:00 p.m."

I guess they did not dig up enough dirt on me to discredit my testimony. Afterwards, we left the courtroom together and had coffee in Lee's office.

Lee asked, "Tina is there anything about your background that could hurt your testimony?"

I said, "Today I am a confessed problem drinker but there is nothing that can be uncovered that could disprove the facts I gave yesterday on the stand."

Lee asked, "Are you sure?"

I said, "Yes, definitely."

Lee asked, "Linda and Joe do you know any information about Tina that could damage her testimony?"

Linda and Joe commented, "The only thing unrevealed is that Tina cheated on her husband the last months she was on the island."

I said, "That is true. However, that had nothing to do with the events of which my testimony was about. Plus, I won't be embarrassed if the prosecutor does bring my cheating into the picture. I never hid that fact. Many people knew it including my husband."

Lee said, "Continue to think while Charlie and I discuss the closing arguement for our case."

Instead of us thinking of dirt, we discussed a little about the past and how the future was fairing. Lee and Charlie joined us once again.

Lee asked, "Couldn't think of any dirt ladies?"

Linda said, "No, no dirt."

Lee said, "Well then, it looks pretty good."

Slyly I commented, "Winner takes all and I get the prize."

Laughing, Linda and Joseph said, "Do we have a prize for you!"

I said, "Sounds like a lot of fun, I hope."

Lee asked, "How about lunch?"

Linda said, "Sounds good to me."

From Lee's office we went to lunch. Charlie and Linda had a craving for pizza. So pizza it was. After lunch we all went back to the courtroom. I could tell that Linda and Joseph were uncomfortable. I guess if I were on trial, unhappy in a job and a marriage, I would be a little uncomfortable, too. Just think, it should be me who is uncomfortable. I am the last person to sit in the 'hot-seat! We were back in the courtroom once again. We all took our places.

Putting his hand on mine lee said, "Relax and just say yes or no. No more than that."

Oh well, I didn't think I looked nervous but I guess I did. It was time to follow the advice of an attorney.

"Please stand." All of the members of the council entered the courtroom. "Please be seated."

The councilman asked, "Now prosecutor do you wish to cross-examine the last witness?"

The prosecutor stood and addressed the council, "At this time we wish to forfeit our cross-examination of the last witness and give our closing argument, if the defense has no objections?"

Lee looked as surprised as I did. He stood and said, "Defense has no objection to concluding this case."

The councilmen acknowledged both parties responses, and said, "The request of the prosecutor is granted."

I was amazed that the Prosecutor was not going to even try to discredit my testimony. He either believes he has this case won or he doesn't want to take the chance of further hurting his case. Well, it's time to see if we won the sympathy that we were shooting for or not.

I sat back in my seat to hear the closing arguments of Lee and the prosecutor.

"I did so, I thought the case over in my head. I really didn't know that much about the case. I only knew that a friend needed help, and I provided that. This case seemed quite petty; however, a lot of cases see a courtroom that most of us don't believe should have entered. As for as I could tell, we should have won a majority vote. But, the Military is a funny place. When you think you're 'scott-free', you get burned. In our case about the only thing that could go wrong is the testimony of the witnesses that were discredited. Under such circumstances we could very well lose.

Lee's argument has been heard. Now is the prosecution's turn. I listened to the theory of the prosecutor. His argument became very pro-military. If this were the 1940's, he would most likely win. However, the 1980's is a whole different era; very different indeed.

The prosecutor concluded his argument and sat down.

The councilman said, "This court is adjourned while council reviews the evidence. Court will re-adjourn when a verdict is obtained."

That concludes this case. Tonight nothing can be said about this case. It is in the hands of the decision makers. I walked over to Lee and Charlie who were telling Linda and Joe not to expect the worst. Lee felt very confident about the out-come.

Lee looked at me and said, "Thanks."

I returned the look with curiosity and commented, "You seem to know the verdict. Could you be a little too confident?"

Lee said, "Well, I've heard the whole case and I feel it would be almost impossible for us not to get a majority vote. The closing statement which the prosecutor cited should hurt his case."

I said, "He didn't make the mistake of further damaging the case and if the council is not pro-military as it was 40 years ago, you could be right. Remember, he had this case won before I testified."

Linda replied, "That's a pretty negative view."

I commented, "Negative maybe, but a factor in this trial. Just don't forget it still can go either way. Don't plan the party before the celebration."

Stopping all the predictions, Charlie announced, "Dinner at the Crab-house. Let's go."

I replied, "Lead the way."

Before departing the courtroom, some friends of Linda and Joe's extended their support towards a positive verdict. One of them, named Bob, said, "Tina, your ex-husband was here today to see you in action."

Trying to hide my amazement, I said, "That was nice of him."

Then we all departed from the courtroom. I picked-up the evening paper on our way to the car. As we drove to the Crab house I looked over the headlines. If there not catchy I don't bother to read the story. However within the couple of days that I've been on the island two murders had been committed. A blonde was the first victim. A brunette was the second victim. The newspapers would like for there to be a connection. However, the police aren't releasing too much detail. I read the name of the detective assigned to the case. He was a friend of mine from years ago.

Interrupting my reading and train of thought, Charlie asked, "Anything good in the headlines?"

I replied, "a little something exciting. By the way did your office have my ex-husband come to court today?"

Lee said, "No. Why do you ask?"

I said, "Just curious why a man who doesn't really want to see or talk to me came to a courtroom to see me 'in action' as Bob stated."

Charlie replied, "Just because two people receive a divorce doesn't put out the flames. Cheer up and let's party."

I replied, "Okay", although, I found his comment very interesting.

Well, dinner was great. It was about time I relaxed; really relaxed.

Before departing for home, Linda said, "See you all in the morning. Tina, if we win tomorrow we have one hell of an evening planned for you. I laughed and said, "Goodnight."

Charlie, Lee and I just laughed along with Linda and Joe. After they exited I asked, "What are your thoughts on the murders in the paper?"

Charlie commented, "you want to solve a murder too while you are here in town?"

I replied, "If I could help I probably would."

Lee said, "So far the police have two corpses both women that are physically different who were supposedly murdered the same way.

It could be two different murders or one murderer who doesn't care who he kills. Maybe something both women did to him. There are a number of reasons out there to be explored. The police have it narrowed to an islander."

I asked, "Isn't that reaching a bit?"

Lee said, "Could very well be."

Charlie suggested, "Maybe you should voice your opinion to the detective handling the case."

I replied, "Being a citizen, I probably should stay out of it."

Charlie said, "You might help open an ally they didn't think about, just like you did for our case."

I said, "Let's end this one first. Let's get out of here. Your ladies would probably like to see you at a decent hour."

We left the restaurant and drove to the hotel. The guys dropped me off. I went in, did a small work-out routine, phoned the office for a 7:30 a.m. wake up call, and went to bed.

Chapter 5

The wakeup call came at 7:30 sharp. I awoke in a sort of a daze. I had had a sexual dream about me and my ex-husband. Since the divorce, the dreams tend to come and go. Oh well, it was time for a shower. Once awake and onto my feet, I could feel the arousal and wetness between my legs. Sometimes I wish a cold shower would relieve the sensations, but for me it only makes me more aroused. Damn! I turned the shower on warm and got in. The shower felt great against my cunt lips. The clitoris was tingling. I could tell it must have been one hell of a dream. If we get a positive out-come in court today, it should be a good eventful night, I hope. Linda seamed sure that I would be surprised, but enjoy is the question? Is long as he doesn't have any diseases, I'm ready for just about anything and anyone. Feeling the tingling in my clit, that was definite! I ignored the calling of my body, since time was short, and continued my shower.

After the shower, I dressed in a suit and high heels. As I was drying my hair, a knock came at the door. I stopped the dryer and opened the door. It was lee and Charlie. I looked at them and said, "You're early. Come in."

Lee said, "We just thought since we have the time that we would invite the detective on the murders case to breakfast so you can talk to him."

I finished my hair at that point, looked at the two of them and said,

"Okay, what's up?" Is there something about this case that you have questions about?"

Lee answered, "Let's just say if you're right, you might not be, going home tomorrow."

I thought to myself, something fishy is going on. Then I threw my cards on the table and said, "You already spoke with the detective. What did he tell you?"

Lee said, "Now, you might be jumping to conclusions."

I said, "I may but I am interested."

So to breakfast we went.

Lee said, "At 10:00 a.m. we will check in at court. I expect a verdict after lunch."

We stopped to have breakfast at the Sizzler Steakhouse. We walked in and sure enough my detective friend was there. We both exchanged Hello's.

Charlie said, "Lee and I will order. You two get acquainted."

I asked, "Didn't you tell them we knew each other?"

Detective said, "No, I did not. The little they know maybe the best."

I replied, "I wouldn't worry about the two men who set this meeting up."

Detective said, "They didn't set this meeting up; I did, two days ago."

Amazed I said, "Sorry. We were talking about the case last night and I just assumed they called you."

Detective said, "That's okay. I wanted to see how you had been since your departure and may I say you look better than ever."

I replied, "Well I straightened my life after leaving this island and set a goal to become a police officer and go forward."

At that point, Lee and Charlie came over and sat with us.

Lee said, "Whatever the two of you say will viewed as confidential and won't be repeated."

The detective relaxed and said, "Thank-you."

I then asked, "What makes you think this suspect is an islander?"

The detective explained, "The last people to see the girls alive said the description of the male they were with was dared skinned and long haired. Sound like any military man you know?"

I replied,,"the guy have a beard or clean-shaven?"

Giving me a strange look the detective said, "You aren't convinced from the description?"

I said, "Well if I were to take a Spanish or deep Italian male and place a dark wig on him, he could just as *WELL* be your men."

Detective said, "But an islander can be distinguished from Italians or Spanish decent."

I said, "True. However, just how close of a look did any one person get of your suspect?"

Detective said, "That is a well put point."

I said, "The establishments visited were on the Waikiki side."

Detective said, "One on this side, one on the Kaneohe side."

I said, "Well, we don't even have that narrowed. Oh! What about the girls. Were they from this side or the other?"

Detective said, "Both from Kaneohe. However, that has no real meaning either. The two women and suspect could have met up anywhere. It is a small island."

I said, "Okay, let's say you're right. The guy is not military."

Detective interrupted, "I'm not saying that he is not of the military. I'm saying we don't know of any tie with the military. What **you are saying could be right."**

I asked, "How do we prevent another murder?"

Detective replied, "We are placing a female and male officer in some of the more popular bars to try and catch the suspect."

I said, "So we have to wait for another murder to be committed."

Charlie interrupted, "I'm **sure** they aren't waiting for another murder. They are trying to prevent another murder."

I looked at Charlie and said, "The words are good for the press, but in all reality when you're short on evidence and description, you're waiting for #3."

I then turned my attention back to the detective and asked, "Right?"

Detective said, "Pretty much."

At that time breakfast arrived. All of **us ate over silence. I believe Charlie and possibly Lee too could not believe** that it was going to take another person's death to gain good evidence against a suspect. As for my detective friend, the evidence he possesses can be linked to one person, however, this is **a** small island and the similarities in people is great. Many people fit the description described.

After breakfast it was time to go to the courthouse. Looking at the detective I said, "you can reach me at the Hyatt Hotel if you want to speak with me again. I'm leaving the day after the verdict."

The detective said, "I will be in touch before you leave."

At the courtroom, the councilman explained, "unlike a regular court of law, all decisions are final. An appeal would do no good in this case since both defendants won't be in the military in 18 months. Therefore, we shall adjourn and after lunch we'll have a verdict. Court adjourned."

Linda and Joe were greeted by more of their friends. One of them said, "See you at the party tonight."

Linda said, "I have purchased the food and booze. However, you can bring your own."

I looked at Charlie and Lee and asked, "What are we going to do now?"

Linda looked at me and said, "You could come shopping with Joe and I."

Lee said, "Since Charlie and I have another case to work on before Friday, go ahead with Joe and Linda. Have some fun."

I said, "Okay. See you at 2:00."

So Linda, Joe and I all went out to the shopping center.

Linda asked, "Are you ready for tonight?"

I asked, "What's there to be ready for?"

Linda said, "Well, we are going to celebrate, eats and drinks."

I asked, "How many people are going to be present?"

She replied, "About 20 if lee and Charlie and their girlfriends attend. And we got you a partner, too. So it's all couples."

I asked, "What's his name?"

Linda and Joe laughed. Linda said, "Don't worry, you'll like him."

While we were shopping, we stopped to eat. Linda and Joe picked up the tab. So far on this trip, I have not paid for anything. I hope they do win since it's costing them a small fortune. After shopping we ventured back to the courtroom.

I asked, "How is my ex-husband fairing?"

Linda replied, "He seems to be doing fine. He doesn't show any sign of problems."

I said, "That's good. Did you ask him to be in court yesterday?"

Linda answered, "We did mention that you were going to be in court for three days testifying. As for him being there, that was his doing not ours."

I asked, "But you made sure he knew who your 'star' witness was going to be?"

Joe said, "Well, he should know. *Any* of your actions do still reflect upon him, divorced or not."

I commented, "so it's better that he is present than absent."

Joe said, "Well."

I interrupted, "never mind."

At the courthouse we met with Lee and Charlie.

Charlie said, "They've reached a verdict."

Linda and Joe said, "Good."

I asked, "Shall we go in and find out the verdict?"

Lee said, "Yes. Let's go."

We all sat down. Minutes later, "please stand." The council members entered the courtroom. "Please be seated."

The councilman said, "Defendants, please stand." Turning his attention to a council member, he addressed, "Has council reached a verdict?"

The councilmember replied, "Yes we have, Sir."

The councilman said, "Please read the verdict."

The councilmember said, "We find all in favor of the defendants."

The councilman said, "Case dismissed. Court adjourned."

Linda and Joe rejoiced with hugs and kisses. Charlie and Lee congratulated each other, then Linda and Joe. Many of Joe and Linda's friends congratulated them, also. I just sat back and watched full of joy myself. It was quite a happy ending for them.

The prosecutor said, "In the military no matter how good or bad a case is represented, nine people have the upper hand."

I said, "It was a hell of a fight."

The prosecutor said, "Yes it was."

Linda looked over at me and said, "Its party time, and you're the woman-of-the-hour."

I said, "You wanted a winner. You pitched the best, and you got what we all wanted, a winner."

Chapter 6

Charlie and Lee dropped me at the hotel. I asked, "Y'all coming to the party with your mates?"

Charlie and Lee both replied, "Yes."

I said, "Okay. Well, I'll see you there."

Charlie asked, "Getting a rent-a-car?"

I answered, "Yes. See you later."

Charlie said, "See you at the party."

Once in my room, it was time for me to prepare for tonight. I **am**-having a hard time getting motivated for a sexually fun evening. My thoughts had shifted from this case to the murders case. I guess one could say I would like to be part of it; however, the danger involved could keep me out of it. Oh well, one day I'll be an officer and have all the excitement. Enough about fantasy land; it's time for reality.

I thought a cold shower would do the trick. After all it usually works. Once in the shower it really felt good. Now I was revived, but not aroused. Hopefully, there will be someone at the party who will help bring that about.

Next, I got dressed in some designer jeans and a red low-cut shirt. Then I said, "Hell! I Might as well go for it."

I took off my bra and changed the shirt to my red tasseled polyester cowboy shirt. Now, I ready for anything.

I walked from my room to the hotel lobby and rented a 5 speed Chevy and took off. I took the scenic route so I could see all of the sites I had seen when I was last here. Hawaii doesn't have much room for growth. Most things were the same. Well, I have goofed-off enough.

After a stop at the store to retrieve some juice that I could consume at the party, it was off to the Chamber's home. I got to the party 45 minutes late, but I didn't care.

I went to the house and Linda greeted me at the door. She said, "Hi Tina, you're late."

I asked, **"Is** my date here?"

Linda said, "Ohhh yes, he's here."

I said, "Then he's had time to relax before I approach."

Linda said, "It's a good thing you were late. We had to talk him into staying."

I asked, "What?? Who the hell did you get?"

Linda said, "Come on. I'll introduce the two of you."

As I walked in, a few people said hello. I returned the hellos.

While following Linda's lead, I couldn't help but think that the 'joke was on me'.

Next thing I heard was Linda say, "This is your date. Enjoy each-other. I don't believe an introduction is necessary."

I guess I shouldn't have been surprised. He would have been my first guess. As Linda walked away laughing, I stood face to face with my ex-husband. I said, "Linda, I'll strangle you later."

Pausing for a moment, I said, "She had to persuade you to stay."

My ex said, "Only because of past experiences was I about to leave. However, that was three years ago; maybe you've changed?"

I said, "Well, I'm not disappointed. I'm really glad to see you.

I was told that you were in court the other day. To say the least, I didn't know what to think or say."

My ex replied, "I was told you were the 'star' witness who was going to 'blow the socks off the prosecutor'. How could I miss seeing that?"

Mellowing out I said, "Why don't we make the most of tonight."

My ex said, "Why not. What would you like to drink . . . Beer? Wine?"

I replied, "Neither. I quit drinking alcohol. I'm wild and crazy as it is. I don't need any extra help."

My ex said, "Oh. I guess that's one change I never expected, but I'm glad to hear it. How's about a soda?"

I said, "I kind of picked up my own. It's **in** the car. Would you like to take a walk?"

My ex replied, "Sure. Why didn't you bring it in with you?"

As we were walking to the car I explained, "I would like to stay sober. Fringing it into that atmosphere, it might get tainted."

My ex said, "You don't trust your own friends."

I replied, "I wasn't too sure I could trust my date, until now."

At the car I opened the door and took out one can from the six-pack.

My ex peered in and asked, "I take it we're going to make a few trips to the car?"

I said, "It depends on how interesting this party gets."

My ex asked, "Bored all ready?"

I replied, "No. I'm interested. However, my interests used to be different from yours."

My ex replied, "Used to be."

Locking the car, we walked back to the party. In the mist of it all, I poured my juice into a glass. A few people noticed.

Charlie asked, "Tina you're not drinking?"

I said, "I know how to have fun without alcohol."

Linda commented, "I bet you d, as she laughed. Enjoy your date."

I slyly said, "I intend too." I walked over to my date and asked, "Would you like to answer 20 questions?"

My ex said, "I would rather dance. I'll change the music."

As he changed the music to something a little more mellow, I said, "I can do both. What about you?"

My ex replied, "as long as you don't get too direct, sure."

I commented, "Well, you can take the 5th on any question which you feel is too direct."

My ex asked, "May I have this dance?"

Recognizing Bob Seager's, "Like a Rock" album playing in the background, I replied with a "yes" after sitting my juice on the speaker.

We began to slow dance as the next song of the album played.

I said, "Well, I know my body looks the best it ever has. What do think of it?"

My ex said, "I like it very much, but I like the mental attitude the best."

Smiling I said, "Thank-you. I see you have been working out.' it looks good."

My ex said, "Yes. It's finally showing."

I asked, "How's work?"

My ex replied, "Pretty good."

I asked, "How's the weather?"

My ex replied, "What? We just came from outside."

I interrupted laughing, "How's about a faster dance?"

My ex said, "You're right. You don't need a substance to bring out your craziness."

We both laughed as the music played. The song "Miami Miami" was a favorite of mine so I kicked my dancing into over-drive. My sexual movements attracted an audience to say the least. After the song ended simultaneous with our steps, everyone applauded.

Now, I was extremely aroused, but a bit worried about being neglected. So I played it cool until I came up with a great idea.

My **ex** said, "Some moves you displayed. Have a drink of your juice while the male attention disappears."

With a smirk on my face, I turned my attention too wonderful taste of the juice that was pouring out of me, and oh! How I would like for him to take a drink of that juice.

My ex said, "Your dancing is really emotional."

I commented, "Sexual would top-off your description."

My ex said, "Uhhh. Yeah. It could."

From across the room Linda interrupted, "Tina! Come here!"

Smiling, I left my date to mingle with the others at the party while I went to see what Linda wanted. I asked, "Yes Linda. What's up?"

Linda asked, "Having fun? You sure look like you are?"

I said, "I told you that I was going to make the most of this evening, and that's what I'm doing."

Linda said, "Sorry about the joke. Joe, Charlie and Lee planned it."

I said, "I'm not really disappointed. However, if you want to have some with the guys, I've got a plan."

Linda said, "Ohhhh!"

I replied, "It's going to take some team-work."

Linda asked, "How juicy is it?"

I answered, "About as wet as my cunt right now."

Linda commented, "The wild side of you is coming out."

I said, "Yes. I think we can induce a lot of fun and a memorable evening for all."

Linda said, "You're still devious."

I asked, "Have I gotten your interest?"

Linda said, "The hell with my interest, you've gotten my participation."

I said, "The first thing we have to do is get the eight other women here to participate. Do you think you can persuade them?"

Linda said, "Give me a couple of minutes."

Before Linda departed, I said, "Tell them all they have to do is follow along."

Linda replied, "Gotcha."

As Linda walked away I—looked towards my date that was looking and walking my way. I smiled as he approached. He said, "It's a nice evening outside. Would you like to take a walk?"

Before I could answer, Linda called from across the room, "Tina! Come over here."

In answer to my ex's question, I asked, "do you accept rain-checks?"

Disappointed, my ex replied, "I'm glad they don't want you the way I do. Go on."

I said, "Excuse me."

Linda said, "Ohm Tina!"

I said, "I'm coming!"

Linda said, "We know that."

Standing in a crowd of women, Linda said, "This is Tina."

I looked at each and said, "I would like to play a game that all of us can play and enjoy. I'll give all the instructions, you just relax and follow."

Linda asked, "are you sure we can get the guys to co-operate?"

Looking at the group, I said, "you ladies know your guys; if everything is sequenced just right, they won't have the chance to say no. Is a matter of fact, they'll be left speechless. Remember, you're his partner." After everyone nodded in agreement, I said, "plain and simple. You are going to be watching your man while he is watching you. At the same time you are listening for a few instructions and apply the moves. Excuse me. Guys! Use the restrooms while you can or forever hold your pieces!!"

Laughter filled the room.

Linda asked, "Why did you do that?"

I replied, "Once we get started there will be no stopping until climax. *We* have to keep all attention on us minute after minute. Let me know when bathroom break is over."

While some of the guys were following my advice, one of the ladies' asked, "How long do we have to take dictation?"

I answered, "Until you hear the words, 'it's all yours ladies'. And another thing, we're the initiators. So everything will be done by us and the guys can't do anything."

Linda asked, "Are you saying they can't touch us?"

I replied, "Exactly! If they were to touch us, I would never get the final statement out. It's a game and the way it ends is up to us. Let me know when the nine of you are ready. I'm going to the bathroom."

After using the toilet, I rejoined the ladies. I said, "In case any one is wondering how one wins the game, it's easy. All you have to do is bring him and yourself to an orgasm. That shouldn't be too difficult, especially after following dictation."

Linda said, "You make it sound so easy."

I said, "Once we get started, you'll see how easy it **is.** Seduction isn't really hard. Come on."

I asked, "Guys are you ready?"

Guys answered, "Yes".

I said, Okay. We need five of you to stand here at an arm's length apart and five over here."

As the guys got into position, I said to the la dies, "The first move is the removal of your shirts and bras immediately following the word 'GO'."

Directing my attention to the guys, I said, "in every game there are rules that must be followed; and you must fully follow the rules.

(1) You cannot use your hands unless requested. So, no hands.
(2) You must be totally submissive and attentive. The lady is in control.
(3) Now, relax and enjoy. Remember, no assistance.
(4) 'Go" marks the start of the game.
(5) Only the ladies know the words that end the game.
(6) The key to winning the game is PATIENCE.

Do you all understand? Are there any questions? It will take about an hour."

Charlie asked, "Will you all play a game of ours, afterwards?"

I replied, "If you'd like. After all fair is fair."

After seeing that there were no more questions, I said, "okay; ladies position yourselves in front of your guys. And guys remember, no helping. Just be attentive. Ready! 'GO!'."

I looked into my ex's eyes and grabbed hold of my shirt and tore open the snaps revealing my round erect breasts. I could hear gasps in the background and saw a much pleasing look on my ex's face.

I instructed, "Now, take off your man's shirt."

Gently, I pulled up my ex's shirt, to his neck and over his head. I viewed a firm built chest with patches of blonde hair scattered about.

After gasping myself, I instructed, "take your fingers, run them from his forehead down his chest to his socks and shoes and remove them."

I placed my fingers lightly on his forehead and ran them over his face down to his neck. My ex's muscles quivered and flexed as I ran my fingers down his chest to his stomach. For a moment I wondered just how much of this could I take, having never performed the act except in my dreams. At his feet, I untied the laces and slipped the shoe and sock off of each foot. I made it a point not to let my eyes leave his, for it was helping to build the sensations in me.

Standing in front of him, I instructed, "now ladies, you Can remove hi$ pants without removing his underwear."

Gently, I placed my fingers on his jeans. I could see from his eyes that he already had an erection that could explode at any time. I unbuttoned the jeans and slowly unzipped the zipper. He gave a sip of relief as I did. I placed my hands on his sides and slid my hands down inside the jeans. By placing the backside of my hands against the jeans and palms facing his skin, I was able to feel his legs twitch and muscles tighten as I proceeded downward to the floor removing the jeans. So far, my ex was reacting quite well and I didn't much care how the rest of the crew was doing. His eyes were glossy with desire as I arose from the floor. I gave a slight smile as I looked into his blue eyes. For only I knew what the, next move was going to be.

I then instructed, "Now ladies, I want you to think back in your pasts to a time when you were ultimately teased without being vaginally touched."

I paused for a moment to allow the ladies to think.

I further instructed, "Proceed to perform those moves either on him or on yourself without touching his penis or your vagina."

I backed up a couple of feet, looked deep into his eyes and took my breasts into my hands and gently massaged them while my hips swayed from side to side. I pinched the taunt nipples. As I pinched, I opened my mouth and swirled my tongue around in circles. While rhythmically swirling my tongue, I slid my fingers over my stomach to my swaying hips and down between my thighs. I closed my mouth and puckered my lips and kissed the air as I moved my hands upward from my thighs, to my stomach, back across the erect nipples, up my neck and through my hair.

I said, "Ladies stop and remove your pants leaving your underwear on your body."

I moved my hands slowly from my sides to my stomach. I unsnapped my jeans and tugged the zipper downward. My ex's eyes were deeply engrossed in my every move. I slid my pants off the same way as I did his; palms in and down. I could feel the juices soaking my underwear.

Afterwards I instructed, "Now you can remove his underwear with your teeth."

I went down to my knees and saw a huge bulge in his underwear begging to be freed. I glanced at him every now and then to see his eagerness of the release. I placed my tongue under the elastic band and pulled the underwear away from his skin allowing my teeth room to grab the material. Once in my teeth, I lifted the material over his penis and down over the shaft. My nose incidentally slid down his shaft causing him to cringe. With underwear still in mouth, I proceeded down his legs to the floor where I removed them. I stood slowly as I longed for the erect purple and pink penis. I had to gasp hard to gain control of myself. His eyes were longing for relief of his full erection.

Then I instructed, "Gentlemen, lie down where you are. Ladies, you are going to dance over your mate to a song while peering into his eyes. At the sound of the music, begin dancing."

I placed the tape in the recorder. I depressed the play button. The song "Chains of Gold" began to play. I strattled my ex's body and moved from toe to forehead in rhythm with the music. When I came to his forehead,. I bent my knees and lowered my wet pantied cunt over his face. I teasingly continued the moves throughout the song, adding hand movements which covered my whole body. The song ended as I was standing in the mist of his body. Since the passion in me was reaching depths I had never felt before, it was time for the 'punch-line'.

I said, "It's ALL YOURS LADIES."

At that point, one could hear ten women simultaneously say, "Touch me!"

My ex tackled me where I stood, ripping my underwear off. His warm wet lips melted against mine as he took his penis in hand and placed it deeply inside of my calling hungry cunt. His tongue was vigorously moving around my mouth as he trusted deeper and deeper inside my body. He slowed down to place me on top of him. From there, I lifted myself to the top of his penis head and quickly down to the base of his penis in preparation for my own orgasm. Three-fourths the way there, with a sudden jerk he shot his come deep inside of me. His entire body flexed and quivered. Moments after seeing his satisfied reaction, I begged for him to flip me over to where my legs were on his shoulders and back against the carpet. As he fulfilled my request, I gripped my legs against his arms and pleaded for him to plunge as deep as he could. His half erect finally reached my button, releasing my long awaited orgasm. He released my legs. We snuggled in each other's arms silently.

After a few minutes, Charlie said, "Tina! On second thought, I don't want to play anymore games with you."

Suddenly, everyone began to laugh.

Linda said, "Ladies! Grab your clothes and head for the showers."

I grabbed my clothes. Five went to Linda's bedroom shower and five went to the guest shower. After emerging from the shower, I couldn't help but smile. I had a lot of fun and fulfilled a fantasy of mine with everyone's. I hope they are all as satisfied as I surely am. While dressing, no one said anything that got my attention. Exiting from the bathroom, I saw that the guys were already dressed and having a drink.

Charlie said, "Tina, Come here!"

I walked over and said, "Yes Charlie."

Charlie asked, "You instructed that game quite well. How many times have you—played it?"

Smiling and looking at my ex I said, "Honestly, once. And this was that one time."

I saw the amazement on all faces, male and female.

With that, I chose to say goodnight.

I said, "Well, this is goodnight to all of you. I hope you had as pleasing an evening as I did. Bye."

Looking at my ex, I asked, "Will you accept my rain-check now?"

My ex replied, "Definitely."

Everyone said goodnight as my ex and I walked out the door.

Walking out to my car, my ex placed his arm around my waist'. He said, "We never did get through the 20 questions you wanted to I leaned up against the car, faced him and said, "I think all of us got 20 answers tonight."

We embraced as we laughed together. With his arms tightly around me, he pulled his face away, with all intentions of saying something.

However, I jumped in and said, "You know, something's are better left unsaid."

He replied, "That's true."

I pulled his face to mine and kissed his soft moist lips. I pulled away and got into the car.

As I started the engine, he said, "It was nice seeing: and being with you again. Good luck."

I drove back to the hotel. I walked inside and headed straight for the shower to wash all of me and not just my cunt as at Linda's. I came out of the shower, dried off, laid my nude body on the bed and thought how nice a reward and bonus I had received from a successful sympathy testimony. It's too bad that we ended in a divorce especially with the magic that we could make. Love is not always enough. It's too bad that that was our decision especially since it feels so right. I turned out the lights and fell asleep feeling very satisfied without a care in the world.

Chapter 7

I awoke feeling very refreshed and relaxed. Since it's my last day in Hawaii, I had to pack all my things. I tossed everything into suitcases. Then, I sat on the bed and thought about last night. I really had fun. I'm going to have to try that game on some of my friends back home.

My train-of-thought was interrupted by a knock at the door. It startled me a bit since I still had absolutely nothing on my body. As I scrabbled through the suitcase for my bathrobe, I said, "just a minute. I'll be right there." I answered the door and to my surprise it was my detective friend, Archie Sweatbaum.

I said, "Hi Archie."

Archie replied, "Hi Tina."

I said, "I'm surprised to see you." Archie came in and I closed the door.

Archie asked, "Did you really think I was going to leave you out of this case?"

I asked, "What do you mean?"

Archie said, "The other day, you implied that you would like to work this case. So, I spoke with the right people and got the okay. However, we have to meet with the General because he has some limitations to put on us."

I asked, "You got me permission to work this case?"

Archie replied, "Yes and the military is paying you for your time."

I said, "I guess I'd better get dressed if we're going to see the General. By the way, how did you get the General to accept a non-police officer?"

I dressed in the bathroom as Archie explained, "We had you're file pulled from when you worked as a security officer at the exchange. The General can hardly discredit a file that his own personnel reviewed and graded. With that and an explanation that we are mainly just looking for the suspect, he agreed. Plus, it is good Public Relations with the outside authorities."

I asked, "So, you haven't ruled-out the possibility that this could be a military man?"

Archie said, "Well, I honestly don't think it is according to the profile, however, it could be a military man's relative. They could visit the establishments on base."

I said, "Nice theory. Well, at least we'll have all establishments covered with someone."

Archie said, "Yeah."

Dressed I walked out and said, "Let's not keep the General waiting."

As we rode to the General's office Archie said, "Your partner has all ready met with the General. You will meet him over dinner tonight. He is a good officer. He and you will work together on looking for the suspect, plus, protecting you."

I said, "Thank you for making that point."

Archie said, "You're welcome. He will also do all paper work in duplicate. I'm sure that's what the General told him."

I asked, "You don't seem too happy about having to work with the General?"

Archie said, "I'm not."

We arrived at the General's office. Once inside, Archie announced us to the secretary. She announced us and showed us into the General's office.

The General said, "Hello Detective Sweatbaum and Ms. Williams. Will you please have a seat?"

Archie and I said, "Hello General." We sat down.

The General began, "I realize that the Hawaii state Police have its way of investigating. However, we have ours, too. I'm going to lay everything out for you and this is the way it will be done. You may ask any questions afterwards."

I thought to myself, "This guy wants no part of this investigation."

The General continuing, "I am going to give you one week to explore our clubs. After one week, your tour will be completed unless you have some proof that the suspect you are looking for is a military man. I want a report on my desk every morning. Ms. Williams this is not a case where you can 'let your hair down'. You and your partner must keep your senses. I will not tolerate any harassment of any kind. You may use your eyes and ears but watch what you say." The General walked to his desk, "after getting your hair changed Ms. Williams go to P.M.O. ID and give them this piece of paper." He handed me the piece of paper. It was an application for an ID card. The General continued, "With your true identity concealed, P.M.O. will give you an ID card allowing you to come and go as you please for one week. You will be paid tomorrow in full for your week's work. You will stay at the Base Inn in room #6. Now, do you have any questions?"

The General sat behind his desk facing Archie and I.

I said, "Sir, I hope you're just as co-operative if it turns out to be one of your men."

The General said, "if that's all, you have your assignments. Good-day."

Archie and I got up and left the office. As we did, I said, "good-day General." We walked to the car. I said, "well, that was short and sweat and to the point. This was un-characteristic of the military. I can tell he's 'Gun-ho' about the whole thing."

Archie said, "Yeah. They would like to see this go away as quickly as possible. Come on. I'll drop you at the beauty parlor. Then I'll retrieve your luggage and check you out of the Hyatt and into the Inn."

As we drove away, I said, "I hope we can prevent #6 from occurring."

Archie said, "I'll take odds on that hope."

We arrived at the beauty parlor and I said, "See you later Archie."

Archie smiled and said, "I'll pick you up in a couple of hours since they're changing you."

We both laughed. Archie drove away and I walked into the parlor. I said, "I'm Ms. Williams I should have an appointment."

The attendant replied, "yes Ms. Williams."

I followed the lady into the back of the parlor. I asked, "Do we have to dye my hair or can we fix-up a wig?"

The attendant replied, "We can do that."

I said, "Great! Show me how to put it on and make me up."

The attendant said, "Fine."

Two hours pretty much flew by with the attendant showing me everything, and me doing it. It wasn't as easy as I thought, but I got the hang of it. I couldn't really get used to all the make-up and being a brunette. Thank-god it was only for a week. Definitely wasn't me or looked like me.

Archie walked into the parlor and asked, "Is Ms. Williams finished?"

I smiled and looked his way, "Yes she's done, here."

Archie tipped the attendant. I said, "thank you for your time."

The attendant replied, "Anything for the General's niece."

Archie and I exited the parlor. Archie said, "You sure look different."

I said, "You're funny."

At the car, Archie said, "It's only for 7 days."

I said, "It's a wig, Archie."

Archie said, "Wig or not you have to wear it whenever you leave the Inn. We don't want anyone to know you're still on this island."

I said, "Well, next stop P.A.O. for ID card."

Archie drove silently. Once there, I got out of the car and said, "I won't be long." I walked to the office. I gave the Lieutenant the paperwork.

He said, "Have a seat."

I sat while he typed up the card information.

Afterwards he said, "Now I need to snap your picture. Come with me." I followed along. "Please sit here." He snapped the photo. "You can sit back over there."

A few minutes later, he said, "Ms. Williams please sign here."

I walked over took the pen and signed where his finger pointed. He said, "thank you."

I watched while he laminated the card. Then he said, "Here is your ID card."

I said, "Thank you."

I walked back to the car.

Archie asked, "All done?"

Getting into the car I said, "Yes."

After driving away, Archie said, "Let's get some lunch off base. Then, I'll bring you back so you can rest until Officer Otto picks you up for dinner."

I commented, "Your Officer has an interesting name."

Archie replied, "It is isn't it."

We didn't talk much about the case over lunch. After lunch, Archie drove me to the Inn. We parked in front of room #6.

Archie said, "Here we are."

I replied, "Yes" and got out of the car. *We* walked to the door and Archie opened it.

Archie said, "Your new quarter's madam."

We entered. It wasn't as nice as the Hyatt but I guess it will have to do. Archie closed the door and walked over to the bed where a folder lie. I sat on the bed opposite him.

Folder in hand he said, "This is a profile of the guy last seen with each victim."

I took a look at the profile and said, "Well, I see why you think it isn't a military man."

The suspect was described as having shoulder-length black hair, dark skinned, mustache, 225 lbs., 6'5". It still bothered me, why he didn't have any sign of a beard.

I asked, "Doesn't it strike you funny that he doesn't have a beard?"

Archie replied, "You're in a warm climate and beards aren't that popular."

I said, "I guess you're right."

Archie said, "I thought you might want to see what your partner looks like, so you don't have dinner with the wrong person."

Taking the picture from his hand I said, "Yes that could help."

I looked at the picture. He was a blonde with a mustache, medium build and definitely cute. I asked, "Does he know what I looked like before?"

Archie answered, "Yes. He saw your picture it the paper from the Chambers' case."

Surprised I asked, "So that's why my identity had to be concealed?"

Archie said, "Yes. You're a big celebrity as yourself. People, who you don't know, know you."

I said, "In that case, I'll only sleep without the wig."

Archie said, "Okay but don't answer the door to anyone else but myself

Archie said, "Okay. Well let me get out of here. Get some rest. Otto should be here around 6 o'clock."

I showed Archie out and replied, "All sixes."

Archie said, "It's just a coincidence." We laughed as I closed the door.

It's been a busy day and the evening is around the corner. I pounced on the bed. I set my watch for 4:30p.m. so I would have plenty of time to get dressed before my dinner date-partner arrived. I fell asleep thinking about the name Otto. I knew it from somewhere

Chapter 8

My alarm sounded at 4:30. I rolled out of bed. I assumed Officer Otto would be here early so straight to the shower I went. I revived myself with cold water first. Then, I showered for the evening. I didn't have too much on my mind. I knew the job at hand and how to handle myself.

After the shower, I fixed my wig and my make-up. After applying the make-up, I was glad I didn't use it all the time. What a mess. No one is going to know who I really am.

I decided I was going to dress comfortably. I pulled out a pair of black dress-jeans and a low-cut blouse. I wasn't out to 'catch' anyone but just in case this case has a sudden change of events I had to be ready. I put my black sneakers on instead of heals. I thought to myself how I really didn't know that much about this case. Hopefully, I can get Officer Otto to talk about it. The newspapers don't say much about the police investigation, either. Only those two women have been murdered and there might be a connection.

A knock came at the door. I looked at my watch. It was 5:26. He is early.

I asked, "Yes. Who is it?"

A voice replied, "Its Officer Otto, Tina."

I opened the door and said, "You're early. Come in."

Officer Otto replied, "Yes. I wasn't sure how much time it would take for me to get here at rush-hour. I like you as a blonde better."

I closed the door and replied, "So do I."

Officer Otto continued, "It is a good disguise. It's too bad that so much publicity came out of the trial that we had to change you."

I said, "I was really surprised to hear that the trial was publicized."

Officer Otto said, "Well, it was the only thing other than that was news-worthy here in Hawaii."

I asked, "Before we get into this case, what is Officer Otto's first name? I can't very well call you Officer Otto if we're working undercover."

Officer Otto answered, "That is true. My name is Robert, Robbie, or Rob whichever you prefer."

I thought to myself for a moment. I used to know a Robbie Otto. He was an old-flame from many years gone by.

Then I said, "Robbie, huh. I used to know a guy by that name. Is a matter-of-fact we were boy-friend and girl-friend back in the eighth grade."

Robbie said, "Well we can talk about ourselves over dinner at the 'E' club. Let's go shall we?"

I replied, "Yes we shall."

We walked out the door to his car.

As we entered the car to ride across the street I said, "I guess we would-not find our long-haired suspect in any other club."

Robbie replied, "Definitely not. He wouldn't be allowed in the Officer's or Staff clubs. I already checked out the dress code for civilians. Men are lucky they allow beards."

As we drove across the street and parked, I asked, "Does it strike you suspiciously that the suspect has no beard to go along with his long hair?"

Robbie replied, "Not many men wear beards in warm climates; so to answer your question it's not so suspicious."

I said, "Well let's have some dinner."

Robbie commented, "Excellent idea."

We laughed and exited the car. We walked into the club together. Robbie showed his ID and signed me in as his guest.

The hostess seated us and said, "You may serve yourselves when you're ready. Nay I get you a cocktail?"

I replied, "Just a large coke, please."

Robbie replied, "I'll have the same. Let's eat first and then I'll explain what we are going to do, plus."

I said, "Since I'm hungry sounds good to me."

Robbie and I went to the buffet. Crab legs really looked good. Being from New Orleans I definitely knew how to tackle them. I loaded my plate with them.

Back at the table Robbie said, "You can go back for seconds."

I laughed and said, "I know. And I just might. Being from New Orleans when it comes to seafood we Cajun women make sure we get enough."

Robbie smiled and said, "Enjoy your dinner."

We ate silently. I really enjoyed myself. I did not need to go back for seconds and neither did Robbie. After dinner, I noticed he was staring at me.

I asked, "Did I make a pig out of myself or is there something else

He commented, "No. It's just that ever since I saw you in the paper I thought that I knew you."

I said, "Maybe you do. However, tell me the game plan and then we'll talk about each other's life."

Robbie said, "Okay. You saw the profile and that's what we are looking for together. If we do spot the man, you would have to use your lady's charm to attract him. I would be your back-up. However, we may just get to enjoy each other's company for 7 days which I don't mind. My wife might but not me."

I replied, "now that the game plan is spelled out, tell me about you."

Robbie narrated, "I'm 25 years old, a wife and daughter each of two years. I know a lot about you from the newspaper. You're from South Florida. I was born in Pensacola Florida."

I interrupted, "Ever been to South Florida?"

Robbie continued, "Yes. I was there for a couple of years. I flunked out of school and my mom sent me back to Pensacola to my father."

I interrupted, "I guess, the year you flunked was your ninth grade year. You lived in Tamarac and I was your 'tomboy' girl-friend in the eighth grade." Waiting for a reply, I could see the amazement in his eyes. I replied, "I didn't mean to shock you, but the story you told me fit my recollection of my first love from 12 years ago. If I'm wrong, I'm sorry."

Robbie said, "No. You're not wrong. Is a matter-of-fact you're 100% correct. I really thought I would never **see** that woman of my past again. And to think, she's sitting in front of me and is my partner for this case."

I interrupted, "since you mentioned it, don't let anyone but you and I know that. Otherwise, we may not be working together."

We both paused for a moment and I said, "Let's go and get a good seat by the door so we can view all who enter the club."

Robbie said, "Okay." He picked-up the bill and paid it as we left the dining room. After paying the bill, Robbie said, "It's time to go to work."

We walked into the disco and found a table facing the entrance. To sat down.

Robbie asked, "how about an orange-juice (oj) straight-up?"

I laughed and said, "I would love one."

Robbie said, "I'll be right back."

Robbie walked to the bar and I watched all the people who walked into the club. I then looked around at every table and saw no male fitting our suspect's description. Robbie came back to the table with our drinks.

Robbie said, "Here you are." He handed me my drink.

I said, "Thank you Sir. Well, our man isn't here yet."

Robbie said, "So I noticed. Well, that gives us more time to get to know each other."

I replied, "Sexual dislikes and likes is the only things we don't know about each other. Since you're a married man that might be all we know but we can hypothesize?"

Robbie said, "Only if you promise to reminisce with me later."

I said, "Okay. Now, we have a killer at least with a description. We have two women killed, but not how. So my question is how?"

Robbie answered, "That information was withheld from the press to prevent any copy-cats. To answer your question, the women were brutally stabbed. If another murder happens, we'll be totally let in on the case and its clues. However, the press will not get anything significant."

I asked, "Where were the bodies found?"

Robbie replied, "Both in their own cars."

I asked, "Were both women known to be promiscuous?"

Robbie replied, "It wasn't mentioned in any of the reports."

I replied, "It sounds like we have two women who did something wrong to upset our suspect."

Robbie commented, "Well, if our killer is a bit deranged, they may have done everything right, too."

I said, "If he is deranged as you imply, we may not find him. However, if his derangement is specific meaning sexually psychotic, we might get lucky. Anyone speak with a psychologist about the case?"

Robbie said, "It wasn't in the reports. Plus, I don't think we have enough evidence linking the murders together."

I commented, "I guess Archie was right. We have to wait for #3."

Robbie said, "I hate to agree but that's what we know."

I said, "Shall we change the subject, since the only thing I've seen walk through that door is short or no haired-men. What about you?"

Robbie answered, "Besides women who are definitely women, you're right. But, it is only 10:00. We have two more hours to watch."

I suggested, "Let's get another of and take a walk outside the walls."

Robbie said, "Okay. You watch and I'll get the drinks."

Robbie walked to the bar. I looked around the room again. He was right; short-haired men and breasted women filled the room. There was no one fitting our profile. Minutes later, Robbie returned with the drinks.

Robbie handed me my drink and said, "Let's mingle."

We walked out and each of us looked around at the crowd as we approached a table. Once settled in the back of the room, we looked over the place again. There was still no sign of our man.

Robbie said, "You promised to reminisce with me, so let's do so."

I said, "Okay. Where do you want to begin?"

Robbie answered, "how about telling me what you thought about me."

I replied, "To start, you were very sweat and gentle. You were there whenever I'd ask for you even after we broke off our relationship. After I moved away, you were still gentle, passionate, and there for me. That's something you don't find in a person when time passes as it did. You were a lot of fun, too. The only thing you didn't know was that the change you got in my personality was all mental and not what you wanted to achieve. You wanted me to change more physically to a women not the 'tom-boy' that I was. But I wasn't in any rush to become a woman. I had many years ahead of me for that change, so I chose to maintain my image even though I felt strongly about you. I think it's your turn."

Robbie said, "I did see changes in you in that short period of time. And you're right, I did want you to be a lot more than you were. I felt competition between the two of us when we were carousing with other people. I guess I was after a more physical change than a mental one. There was an instant attraction between us, at least that's the feeling I received. Plus, you were a challenge. With all that, it was hard to stay away from you. And you had a **kiss** that I really enjoyed. So I guess, we felt the same about each other just never said it."

I said, "I always thought it was your **kiss** that made it so enjoyable. Anyway, it sounds like we definitely had a driving passion for one another. It's funny how I'm feeling 12 years ago all over again. But I guess that's the beauty of reminiscing; otherwise, it wouldn't be worth a damn."

An announcement sounded, "Last call for alcohol!"

Robbie said, "Well, it's close to quitting-time. Now, how's about a real drink?"

I replied, "No thanks. I quit drinking a few years ago and I'm going to keep it that way. But I will take another oj."

Robbie smiled and said, "You got it."

As Robbie walked to the bar one last time, I looked around the room at everyone. No sign of our suspect. I have to admit some of the women in here could ID as our suspect with just one flaw. At least I've enjoyed my company. Robbie came back with the drinks.

Handing me my drink, he said, "Here you are sweetheart."

I commented, "12 years ago, yes. Now you have a wife and a child."

Robbie laughed and said, "I hope in the next 6 days I don't forget that."

I asked, "Are you sure you hope you don't forget or that you do forget?"

Robbie said, "We'll just have to let nature take its course, won't we?"

We both laughed seriously.

I suggested, "Since this place is clearing out why don't we call it an evening?"

Robbie replied, "Sounds good to me. Let's go."

We got up and walked to the car. I fumbled around in my purse for the keys to the room. After finding them, Robbie opened the car door and drove us across the street. At that point, it was time to say goodnight.

I looked at Robbie and said, "Well, it has been an interesting evening."

Robbie replied, "Yes. It has indeed and the next few are going to be just as interesting if not better."

I said, "thank you for a nice uneventful evening and some beautiful reminiscing. I'll see you tomorrow."

Robbie said, "Yes you will. If anything turns up it will be earlier than you think. Get some sleep."

I exited the car and said, "Goodnight Robbie."

He said, "Goodnight and sweat dreams."

I closed the car door and walked to the Inn door, unlocked and turned on the light. Robbie watched as I did. I waved goodbye. He waved back.

Once inside, I wondered if he wanted to **kiss** me goodnight as much as I wanted to kiss him. On this job, I must remember to keep my attention tuned to my duties and not my passion for an ex-boyfriend. However, those lips were once very gentle and smooth tasting. It is hard keeping that off my mind. I'm pretty sure it wasn't easy for him either.

Oh well. Finally, it was time to get rid of this wig and make-up. I pulled the wig off, let my hair down and took off my clothes. Then, I hopped into a warm shower. The warmth of the shower reminded me of Robbie's warm body against mine when we were 'making out' on the grass together years ago. Just then the passion moved me. It was time for a finger-fucking. I closed my eyes and placed my index finger against my clit and massage it lightly. Once the lips parted, I slid my finger inside. With my thumb, I continued to massage the clitoris while plunging my index finger teasingly inside of me. I began to lose control and call Robbie's name. I then slid my middle finger in also. Thrusting my fingers back and forth quickly with thumb still tickling the clit, an orgasm ran through my body. I hope I didn't wake the neighbors as loudly as I cried Robbie's name when my orgasm arose. Afterwards, I continued my shower. I was quite relaxed as I got out of the shower and dried off with a towel. As usual, I slid my naked body into bed where I wished Robbie laid waiting for me. This case was all ready difficult and now it just got a lot more difficult.

Chapter 9

Next morning, I awoke feeling as aroused as I did when I went to bed, so it was back to the shower to calm the anxiety. The shower felt really good against my body. It was warm and delightful just like the dream I awoke from. I switched the shower-head to its three-way jet massage. The water tingled against my clit while at the same time it excited my anis. It felt as if I was being plugged by two men at the same time. It was quite an interesting feeling. I could have stayed in the shower all day enjoying the feeling but it was time to bounce back to reality if I was going to get anything done.

After the shower, I decided to dress in some shorts and explore the base a little. With two beaches and a pool, I could lie out and enjoy Hawaii's sunny days. After dressing, I placed my wig on my head, grabbed a towel and my purse and headed for the door. As I opened the door, I was taken-back to see Robbie standing in front of me.

Robbie said, "Looks like you're going somewhere. Well, I hate to disrupt your plans, but #3 has turned up. Put some less revealing clothes on and let's go."

Disappointed I asked, "Would you like to come in?"

Robbie smiled and said, "Okay."

He came in and I pulled out a pair of pants from the drawer along with a pull-over shirt. Instead of getting dressed in the bathroom, I disrobed and dressed in front of Robbie. I guess my mind was still on last night's dream.

Robbie asked, "I take it you were going to the beach?"

I replied, "Yes I was; however, I would rather see the murder and speak with the psychologist. I'm ready. Let's go."

Robbie commented, "I hope you don't get undressed in front of all of your partners."

On the way out the door I said, "Only those I'm interested in."

Entering the car I changed the subject. I asked, "Where's the crime scene?"

Robbie answered, "Near the club 'First Step'."

I replied, "I've been there a couple of times. How long has the investigating team been there?"

Robbie replied, "About an hour. Archie wants to fill us in on the whole case. It seems this time no one is quite sure who she Left with."

We arrived at the scene. Robbie and I got out of the car and walked towards Archie.

Archie said, "Hello Tina and Otto. Well, meet #3."

Archie pulled back the zipper on the bag. As Robbie and I looked Archie described, "she's a brunette, 130 lbs., 5'10", white female. We've spoken with the bartenders of the last evening. They said she was mingling with military men as well as islanders. No one saw actually who she left with."

Robbie commented, "That widens the scope a bit. What about other evidence? Does she tie in with the other M.O.'s of the other girls?"

Archie replied, "She was killed by stab wounds; also, was left in her auto. She has some stains on her clothing which we have yet to checkout."

I asked, "Is the psychologist here?"

Archie said, "Yes. He's right over there. The two of you speak with him and I'll have a report for you tonight at dinner. See you at six."

I said, "Let's talk with the Dr. Robbie."

Ps we walked over to speak with the Dr. I saw the coroner's wagon drive away with the body. Robbie and I approached the Dr.

Robbie said, "Hello Dr. I'm Officer Otto and this is Ms. Williams."

The Dr. replied, "Hello Officer Otto and Ms. Williams. Sweatbaum has asked me to fill you in on the details. Would you like to have lunch?"

Robbie and I replied, "Yes."

We walked over to a fast-food restaurant and ordered. We sat in the very back away from all else. While eating, the Dr. filled us in. The Dr. said; "Today's victim appears to have been murdered the same way as the others. We'll know more after the autopsy. We have a physical profile of the suspect as you know. According to the evidence, there's a strong possibility that he's taking revenge of some kind out on women."

I interrupted, "Excuse me. Could it possibly be sexually related?"

The Dr. answered, "In the other cases, there is no sign of sexual contact."

I asked, "What about the weapon? Do we know anything about it?"

The Dr. replied, "The knife is thin and long. It is not a steak knife. It is more like that of a pocket knife."

I asked, "So the wounds are of average size and length?"

The Dr. said, "That's the clincher. If it's a pocket knife, it is not a standard one. Some of the wounds in the two victims' are up to nine inches long. All evidence shows that the nine inch wounds are single cuts."

Robbie asked, "Could the nine inches have some significance?"

I Added, "Maybe a sexual significance?"

The Dr. said, "that's a good point, we just aren't really sure. The majority of wounds found on both victim's are pinpointed to the abdominal below the rib cage. No wounds in the lower areas."

Robbie asked, "That's the only area stabbed?"

The Dr. said, "That's enough to kill anyone. Plus, the knife being nine inches in length can go straight through the body. Many of the wounds did just that."

I asked, "So what makes him act normal until he and she are alone? And what could possibly trigger the attack?"

The Dr. said, "Well, the emphasis on the abdomen. Therefore, there must be something about the area that is the problem. Or as in your sexual hypothesis, it could be the only area not touched. We know the guy has a grudge against women and the abdomen area of their bodies. For our perpetrator, it could be an abortion, miscarriage, or even a death of someone else. All I can really say is that he isn't leaving many clues to identify him and that more women are in line to be next."

I commented, "Well, our psycho is okay until he's alone with a woman which must mean that that's not very often."

Robbie asked, "What do you mean?"

I said, "Well, add it up. All three girls are murdered at night and so far every other day. Now, if he was able to be alone with a woman every day, we would have a death every day."

The Dr. replied, "Maybe true or something happens every other day that a woman's involved in that he doesn't like."

I said, "Well then, why go to a bar, pick up a no body and kill her?"

Getting up from the table the Dr. said, "Well you now know what we know. I've got to get back to the office. Have a good day and good luck."

Robbie and I said, "Goodbye Dr. Williams."

As the Dr. exited, Robbie said, "You look as puzzled as the rest of the force."

I commented, "I am. We have a lot of ideas but nothing concrete."

Robbie said, "Sometimes we have to work only with ideas. Where can I drop you? I have to take my wife to the doctor's office in an hour. Let's go."

As we left the restaurant I replied, "I guess I'm the only one who finds it easy to forget you're married?"

As we got into the car Robbie replied, "As of late, you're not the only one."

I decided just to let that comment slide even though deep within me I knew how much I wanted to have him for myself.

I replied, "The Inn. I have to change, again."

Robbie said, "I wish I had time to watch."

Returning to the base Inn I turned to Robbie and said, "See you and Archie tonight."

I kissed him on the check and got out of the car. I didn't bother to look back as he drove away. I was hoping that the other person he spoke of was himself who felt the way I was feeling.

I entered the room, changed, grabbed my purse and towel and took off for a journey around the base. After seeing the body and speaking with Dr. Williams, I needed to think. So out the door and on my way I went.

I walked around the base just looking at all the beauty and peace that was about me. I thought to myself how many of today's youths take this for granted. Only thing I've learned over the years is since no one knows when time will end you'd better stop and smell the roses.

Time slipped by quickly. I got back to the Inn at 3:57. I had two hours to shower, dress and make-up for tonight's venture.

I stripped down to nothing and put my bare little body into the shower.

I lukewarm shower did the trick of cooling me down and waking me up for my evening out. After the shower, I combed-out my wig. I sat my make-up on the counter for me to apply. I went to the drawer and pulled a pair of pants and a satin western-shirt from the drawer. I wasn't in the mood to dress fashionable for tonight, especially just to see Robbie and Archie. Plus, I was tired. Well, I had everything laid out for me to put on.

With everything laid out it was time for me to put it all on. I put my make-up on and then the wig. Now it was time to get dressed. After dressing I looked in the mirror and said, "all but the hair and make-up, this is me." I laughed when I thought about it.

Besides being tired I was a little disappointed that the police still didn't have much to go on. I really hope that Archie can tell us more.

I tried to switch my thoughts to a brighter subject. However, even my desire for Robbie was a bit tired. Oh well, I've always brightened up when company was around.

A knock came at the door. I thought to myself, "It must be Robbie."

I opened the door smiling. To my surprise it was Archie not Robbie.

Archie said, "You'd better watch yourself. Robbie is a married man. May I come in?"

Archie entered. I asked, "What makes you say that?"

Archie said, "I've known you for a long time and that look in your eyes and smile, spells desire. Just be careful. He had to take her to the doctor's today to be examined for a possible pregnancy."

I said, "Thanks for the information."

Another knock came at the door. I opened it. It was Robbie. I said, "Hi Robbie. Come in. I think you know Archie." Robbie entered.

Robbie said, "Yes. I think we've met. Hi Archie."

Archie asked, "How's the wife?"

Robbie answered, "It's just an infection. Give her a week, she'll be back

Archie said, "That's good. The two of you ready for dinner?"

I said, "Yes. Let's go."

Guess I was kind of pissed off at Archie for what he had said, however, adultery is still frowned upon by a chosen few. I even don't care for it; however, I couldn't ignore the passion building within me either. I need to play it cool until Robbie makes the moves even though it's not my personality to wait.

We left the room, entered the cars and drove across the street to the club.

Robbie asked, "You're kind of quiet tonight, is there anything wrong?"

I answered, "No. I took a long walk around the base after you left and didn't return until 4:00. So I'm just a little tired."

We got out of the car and met with Archie.

Robbie commented, "It's reasonable that you're tired."

I said, "Thanks for understanding."

Archie said, "Let's go in, relax and I'll tell you the news."

I said, "How thrilling."

Robbie suggested, "Cheer up Tina."

I just smiled as Robbie signed Archie and I into the club. The hostess seated us and took our drink orders. I ordered a coke. Archie and Robbie ordered screw-drivers. I would have loved to have told Archie where he could stick an actual screw-driver. I shouldn't be pissed off because someone saw through me; I have to cheer up as Robbie said. After dropping off the drinks, the hostess said, "Help yourselves whenever you're ready."

We replied, "Thank you."

Archie asked, "You want the news now or after dinner?"

I replied, "Now is okay."

Archie said, "The stab wounds were made by the same instrument. Each was nine inches deep in some areas. The stains on her clothing were of alcohol and food and make-up. The make-up was not hers. However, mingling in a bar it could have come from anyone. All blood was of the victim's. Now, for the bad news. We still have no fingerprints. None were found in the car or outside of it. Witnesses claim she mingled with military men as well as islanders. However, our profiled suspect was identified as being seen with her approximately 30 minutes before she apparently left."

I interrupted, "Sounds like no one knows just who she left with?"

Archie said, "That's right. There are no eyewitnesses who actually saw her leave. However, witnesses did claim that when our suspect approached her it was like they knew each other."

Robbie interrupted, "so we have a corpse who mingled with military men and who knew the suspect. So who are the witnesses to this?"

Archie answered, "One military man is a witness. There were two who conversed with her who left the bar at about the same time our victim left. I have a new profile of him that the two of you need to be on the look-out for."

I said, "I hope you realize that one 'jar-head' looks like another."

Archie said, "I never said he would be easy for you to find."

I asked, "So now we have to look for two different people?"

Archie replied, "Yes, but I mainly want you to concentrate on locating this guy. Let's face it, if a long haired male walks in here, you'll know it."

I asked, "What if we do locate this witness?"

Archie suggested, "Treat him like you would our suspect. Play it cool. You never know, he might be our man. Set up a time to meet with him and we'll prepare from there."

Robbie said, "That's putting Tina at a high risk."

Archie stood and said, "She can handle it. Let's eat. Besides, she'll be wired in case anything should happen."

I commented, "Great."

We got up to eat. It was boiled shrimp and lobster night. I filled my plate even though my appetite was small. Back at the table, we all ate in silence. After we finished, Archie and Robbie ordered two more screw-drivers and I a coke.

Archie broke the silence, "So Robbie is the wife going to have a little Robbie?"

Robbie answered, "No. Where did you get that idea?"

Archie said, "One of the girls in dispatch said something to that effect."

Robbie said, "Definitely not. She claims she's not ready for another, so I'm still waiting."

I replied, "Some women want to get it over with as soon as they can afford it."

Robbie said, "I don't know why she wants to wait, she just does."

Archie said, "Well, good luck when she does give you the go ahead. Now, let me let the two of you get to work but first, a toast for luck." We all lifted our glasses and said, "Here, here."

Archie said, "Good night" as he picked up the bill.

As he walked away I said, "Good night Archie."

Archie said, "Before I go, you have to be in the General's office at 10:00 a.m. tomorrow. Bye."

Archie walked away and I commented, "Another nice chat with the General.

I grumbled, "Yeah, yeah."

Robbie said, "I have this aching feeling that Archie said something that pissed you off. Am I right?"

I replied, "Since tonight's conversation was over your wife and kids, one might ascertain such."

Robbie asked, "Are you going to let it ruin our evening tonight?"

I answered, "No. However, looking for a military man is going too. Speaking of which, we never saw the profile."

Just then, Archie walked back to the table. Archie said, "Hi guys. I forgot something."

Archie handed me the picture. I studied it and gave it to Robbie.

Archie said, "Now, I'm gone." Archie exited again.

I asked, "Would you say, he has something else on his mind?"

Robbie replied, "He sometimes gets that way when we can't figure out a case."

I asked, "Shall we go watch the crowd?"

Robbie replied, "Sure."

We walked out into the lobby. Looking around, I couldn't spot anyone right off the bat who matched the description of our witness.

Robbie suggested, "Let's look inside the disco."

I replied, "Right behind you."

Looking around I suggested, "Let's split up. Meet you at the bar."

Robbie said, "Fine."

I had to look around closely at the men since most of them could have been our witness. After a very observant search, I met Robbie at the bar.

I asked, "Any luck?"

Robbie replied, "No. Here's your oj."

Handing me my drink I said, "me either."

Robbie said, "I know. I was watching you. Let's go outside and sit down."

As we walked I said, "You're supposed to be watching for the witness."

As we sat down at our table from last night Robbie said, "You're half right. I'm supposed to watch you too. Besides, I'm more interested in you."

I said, "We have a job to do. Besides, you know all about me. What more do you want?"

Robbie asked, "What do you like sexually?"

I answered, "That's pretty direct. What about your wife?"

Robbie said, "I can talk. I'm just not supposed to touch."

I replied, "It sounds like you would if you could."

Robbie said, "With the right woman, maybe."

I said, "Well since you did ask, when it comes to work I like to get the job done as soon as possible; however, from a sexual standpoint I enjoy taking my time very much."

Robbie asked, "Would you care to elaborate?"

I said, "Picture this. Sex is a circle. From your first penetration onward, that circle begins to grow and so does your knowledge. With every penetration, you learn something new about yourself and the other person. The circle never shrinks and you never become a virgin again either. So, I for one lets my circle continue to grow and educate me."

Robbie said, "I've never thought of sex quite that way. Personally, I feel that when the moments right, one should go for it."

I asked, "Is that with anyone or just your wife?"

Robbie replied, "That would be 'letting the cat out of the bag'."

I said, "Yes, but you seem to be a pretty faithful husband."

A voice sounded, "Last call for alcohol!"

I looked at my watch and said, "It's only 10:30."

Robbie replied, "They close when they're not doing much business."

I asked, "Are you going to comment on my last statement?"

Robbie said, "I haven't cheated on her, yet. But I can't say that I won't. Let's face it, no one's perfect today. We just all try to be."

I commented, "That's an interesting reply. Well, since this place is closing, shall we go?"

Robbie said, "Yes. I'll drop you across the street."

We left the club for the night. As we walked to the car I said, "remember, we have to be' in the General's office at 10:00."

Robbie said, "Yes for another listening session."

I laughed at his reply as we entered the car. We drove across the street.

I asked, "Are you okay to drive?"

Robbie said, "Oh yeah. I was just thinking."

We parked in front of the room. I asked, "Anything on your mind you'd like to share?"

Robbie said, "Honestly. You're on my mind and have been all day and night."

His words might not have been a cue but I decided I'd waited long enough. I wanted very much to feel how much his kiss had changed over the years. When our lips met, I slid my body next to his. That old feeling awakened inside of me. I ran my fingers through his straight blonde hair as the passion filled me with each stroke of the other's mouth and back around our tongues. His arms gripped around me pulling me even closer to him. We were both beginning to let our emotions run away when I had to pull away, otherwise, he would not make it home tonight.

Robbie said, "You don't have to stop. I wanted that as much as you. And I want your body as much as you want mine."

I said, "Yes, I know all of that, too. However, we have an early appointment and you have a sick wife. Like you said when the time is right, it will happen. But that time isn't now. Good night darling."

I got out of the car. I knew he was disappointed, but he's smart enough to know that I'm right, too. I didn't look back for I knew my body would insist on me inviting him inside, and that could be detrimental to his marriage. I opened the door, walked in, and closed it. I leaned against the door until I Heard him drive away. I was kind of mad at myself for kissing him. However, it was going to happen sooner or later. Definitely, before this case was over.

I walked over to the bed and laid my fully clothed body on it. From there I just stared at the ceiling. It was a funny feeling, one part of me was mad and the other was aroused by the passion that unearthed in both of our bodies after so many years apart. However, I would mind if another woman seduced my husband. Therefore, he knows that I want him so he'll have to make the seductive moves not me. And that I will not pull away from.

Chapter 10

A new day was upon me. I awoke with a splitting headache. That's what I get for going to bed mad. I got up and took some aspirin. Looking in the mirror at myself, it was time to unclothe and hit the shower. I remembered while undressing that eaten in drunken-stupor I had never fallen asleep with my clothes on. I guess my guilty conscience got to me. Oh well, hell! It's a new day. I took off the wig and turned on the shower. As the water warmed, I combed the wig. Taking off my watch, I noticed that it was 9:15. We had to be in the General's office in 45 minutes. I hurriedly jumped in the shower, soaped, rinsed my body and got out. While drying off, I picked out some clean clothes to wear. Just then a knock came at the door.

I said to myself, "Damn!" Then I causally said, "Who is it?"

Robbie's voice sounded, "It's me, Robbie. We have a meeting in 30 minutes with our favorite Boss."

I said, "I'll be right there."

I quickly put my underwear, pants and a shirt on. I definitely didn't need to further lead my partner on. I walked to the door and opened it.

Robbie said, "I see you aren't ready." He entered and closed the door.

I replied, "Whatever gave you that idea."

Both of us laughed, and Robbie said, "Go finish getting ready. I won't mind watching."

I walked over to the bathroom mirror to put on my make-up and the wig. But first, I had to brush away a bad taste in my mouth. Then, I tucked my shirt into my pants. I put the make-up and wig on. Robbie walked up behind me as I was finishing.

Putting his arms around my waist, he said, "I like you better with no make-up and as a blonde. Definitely."

I turned to face him and asked, "Do you really?"

He pulled me to his lips and we kissed. The passion I felt last night immediately returned. As the kiss began to get more passionate, I pulled away.

I said, "I we have a General waiting on us."

I walked away, sat on the bed and put my sneakers on.

Robbie sat down beside me, turned my face to his and said, "soon, neither one of us will be able to pull away. The desire we have for each other is going to over-ride any order."

I put my hand on his face, kissed him lightly and said, "Yes. I know that too. But, it won't be today. Let's go."

We both got up from the bed and walked out of the door to the car.

In the car I said, "Don't let me forget to ask about my pay. Do you have the evidence reports?"

Robbie replied, "Yes. They are in that folder on the seat." As we drove to the office, I read the contents of the folder. Robbie commented, "You'll find that it doesn't say much more than what we knew yesterday. I see nothing unusual or noteworthy."

Getting out of the car at the office building, I said, "so we're walking into the General's office with nothing except, one of his men may have seen something? But, you have nothing that actually ties the military to the murders?"

Walking into the building Robbie replied, "I'm afraid that's all."

I said, "He's going to remind us that we only have a couple of days to go."

Robbie said, "Well he gave us a week and I intend to hold him to it. Ms. Williams and Officer Otto to see the General, please."

The secretary announced us. She said, "Through those doors."

I said, "Thank you." Robbie opened the door and we entered.

Robbie and I said, "Hell", General." Closing the door, we sat down.

I said, "Here is the report on the 3rd victim."

The General said, "Yes. I heard your suspect is still profiled as an islander."

Robbie said, "Yes Sir. So far as we know. However, now we're looking for one of your men who were also seen with our 3rd victim."

The General said, "So what you're telling me is that one of my men might know something."

Robbie said, "The victim and the serviceman were said to have left the bar at about the same time. Therefore, he might have seen or even heard something. Plus, he might be able to give us a better description of our islander suspect."

The General implied, "I take it, you will be circulating a bit more to find this person."

Robbie replied, "If we do spot the serviceman, we'll set up a time to meet with him and question him accordingly."

The General said, "I don't want the serviceman questioned in public."

Robbie said, "Then we'll have to wire Ms. Williams and after they leave the bar for some peace and quiet, we'll take him in for questioning."

The General said, "I would like the meeting between Ms. Williams and my man set up for the next night. Then, I will have time to put two of my officers on the surveillance detail and with you for questioning."

Robbie said, "That was going to be my next suggestion, Sir."

The General said, "Well, if that's all, I'll expect to hear from you in a day or two. By the way, Ms. Williams this belongs to you along with an open airline ticket back to Florida." I took the paperwork from his hand. He said, "I'm sorry it's late. Have a good day."

I said, "Thank you General. Good-bye."

Robbie said, "Good-bye General. We'll be in touch."

Robbie and I stood and walked out of the office.

Leaving the building Robbie asked, "Want me to take you to cash your check?"

I said, "You can drop me at the PX and I'll walk back to my room. That way you can get what appears to be some necessary sleep."

Robbie smiled and said, "Yeah. The wife was tossing and turning in pain much of the night, so I didn't get much sleep."

I'e got into the car and drove to the PX. I replied, "That was a pretty impressive pitch that you told the General."

Robbie laughed and said, "Well, I told you I wasn't ending this case until we ran out of time. When we do locate the serviceman, the procedure I described is the way we'll do it. The wiring is for your protection even though we may not need it. This guy might not know anything or may have been too drunk to remember. However, the General need not know the negative aspect of this case."

Arriving at the PX I replied, "I'm glad you don't want to lose your partner."

Robbie said, "Definitely not. I have plans for us. See you tonight."

I smiled and got out of the car. I said, "Tonight." I walked into the exchange. I pulled out my ID card and cashed the check. Now I have some money. It was time to get some lunch. I had a hotdog and chips. Not much of a lunch, but if you consider I'm going back to the room for some more sleep, it was enough. Back at the room, I stripped off my clothes and laid down on the bed for a nap. I set my alarm for 4:30. I took off the wig and slid my nude body under the covers and eventually fell asleep.

4:30 came much too quickly. I turned off the alarm and felt a lot better than I did this morning. I was pretty relaxed considering the case just got a little more risky. If I use my head, I shouldn't encounter anything I can't handle. Oh well. It is time to roll out. I combed out the wig and put my make-up on. I decided to wear the same clothes I had on a couple of hours ago. That made things pretty simple. I put the clothes on and some perfume just in case I met up with our witness tonight. Then, I put on the wig. Afterwards, I sat on the bed and flipped on the television to see what was on. It was only 5:15 and I knew I had some time to kill. So I caught the last part of a military show. A few minutes after the show ended, a knock came at the door. Robbie's early again. I approached the door and asked, "Who is it?"

Robbie said, "It's me, Tina."

I opened the door. I said, "You're early again. Are you that hungry?"

Robbie laughed and said, "Archie called. He wants to see us at the steakhouse for dinner. He said it was important, so get your things and let's go."

I said, "Okay. I'm ready."

I grabbed my purse and turned off the television. I said, "Let's go."

Robbie said, "Let's."

We walked out the door and to the car. I jokingly said, "Let's not keep the 'preacher' waiting."

We got into the car and Robbie began to laugh at my comment. He said, "I don't blame you. I don't particularly like being judged by other people either. I feel what I do is my business."

Is we drove to the restaurant, I replied, "He's only covering our asses. And I may add, trying to keep our minds on this case."

Entering the parking lot Robbie said, "I could see the man's point if I were known to play-the-field behind my wife's back. However, I'm not known for that at all."

We got out of the car and I said, "His statements might be more directed towards me and not necessarily you. I'm afraid I do have somewhat of a reputation for getting a man when I want one."

Walking into the restaurant Robbie commented, "It's not hard for a woman like yourself to get what she wants."

I said, "Shut up."

Robbie asked, "Are we under esteemed tonight?"

I sternly said, "Use your mouth to order while you can."

Robbie commented, "I'll have the special, medium rare; bake potato, salad and coke. Looking at me he said, "It's your turn."

Robbie looked at me with a big smile on his face. I could only smile back at him instead of getting angry. Sometimes the truth of my past does hurt. I ordered, "I'll have the same as he." Robbie reached for his wallet to pay, I said, "you can put that away. I'm picking up the tab."

Robbie said, "But I get reimbursed."

I commented, "Your old 'nickname' sits well with you even today. Put your wallet away." I pulled out twenty-five dollars and paid the tab. We then walked over to where Archie was sitting. I couldn't help but notice that he was full of laughter.

Once at the table, Robbie asked, "What's so funny?"

Archie said, "The way you two were arguing. Just like a husband and wife. HAHAHAHAHAHAHA."

Robbie and I sat down. I asked, "So, what's this little get-together about?"

The waitress took the trays away and our ticket number. I said, "thank you." She left and I switched my attention to Archie and said, "It's your turn."

Archie said, "after that spat, I don't know whether you're going to like this or not but it's an order. The other day Tina you said that the murders seemed to be happening every other day. If that's the case, tomorrow I want the two of you together waiting for a call from me, so we can examine the evidence of #4 quickly. Tonight would be the night he gets #4 if he stays on this pattern. So whenever we find the body, I want to be able to reach both of you either by telephone or radio. Robbie, when you get to the Inn, I want you to call in. I'll let you know if we have anything at that time. So tonight decide; "Three steaks, medium rare." The waitress sat the food on the table. She asked, "Will there be anything else?"

We all replied, "No."

Archie continued, "What you're going to do tomorrow and where I can reach you. That's all. Let's eat, I'm starved."

We all sat and ate our meals. After we had finished, I asked, "Do you really think he'll strike again?"

Archie disgustedly said, "The *guy* doesn't have much to lose. We don't have any more evidence with the 3rd murder than we did with the first. So yes, I think that he'll strike again and again until we get him when he slips." Laying a dollar on the table, he stood and said, "Good luck on your search tonight for our witness. Good night." Archie left.

I commented, "His mood fits this case well. It's not a cheery thought to think that we're going to stumble across #4 tomorrow."

Robbie said, "Well, let's feel bad when that time comes." He laid a five on the table and said, "Let's go."

I commented, "Deep in thought again." We walked out of the restaurant.

Robbie said, "The guy's only killing women, so I have nothing to fear."

I said, "That's a nice thought."

As we got into the car Robbie said, "It was wasn't it."

I looked at him as we drove away and said, "All of a sudden, you're unreal."

Driving back to the base Robbie just laughed. Once at the club, I got out of the car and said, "Death isn't exactly a laughing matter."

Walking into the club, Robbie just smiled as he signed me in as his guest. I said, "Get us some oj and I'll grab a seat."

Robbie said, "Okay."

I found a table close to the table we usually sit at. The club wasn't busy, yet. I looked around and saw no sign of our suspect or witness. Robbie walked back to the table.

Robbie said, "Here you are. Did you spot our friends?"

I took the drink from his hand and said, "No. Did you see anything I might have missed?"

Robbie said, "No. I was just curious to see if you were doing your job?"

I stood and said, "I'm going to take a walk through the disco. Fit here and get rid of that attitude?"

I walked away and he still wore that shitty little grin on his face. I walked into the disco and looked around closely. I thought as I observed the crowd, the witness could be our suspect minus a few pounds of course. However, the rest of his physique didn't add up. No long hair or dark skin or mustache. Matter-of-fact our witness is rather a plain type of guy which makes it harder to find him. Oh well. After walking through the disco with no luck, I stopped at the bar and ordered a screw-driver for Robbie and another oj for myself. I walked back to the table with drinks in hand. I looked at Robbie and asked, "Want a screw?"

Robbie smiled and said, "I sure do." I handed him the screw-driver beverage.

Robbie commented, "That's not exactly what I had in mind."

Changing the subject I asked, "What do we talk about tonight?"

Robbie said, "Well, we can do some island exploration tomorrow. How would you like to go to see the Bay tomorrow?"

I said, "Sounds good to me. Fell, that was easy. So I'll see you at 9:00 a.m. sharp, right?"

Robbie said, "Sure."

I said, "I guess your attitude is correct since we can't save every life out there."

Robbie said, "I have to admit when I first became a cop that wasn't easy to accept. Every time you turn around, you get accused of not doing enough. I don't know why so many people think this job is like the movies; little hard work and the case is solved. It's just not that easy."

I replied, "That's very true. Police work is a career that a person takes for recognition rather than the money. You're always on the move and you'll always be a target. If a bullet doesn't get you, the press will. You have to go in with pride and leave with it."

Robbie asked, "Knowing how this job **is,** why do you want to be a cop?"

I answered, "Because I possess knowledge that can help people of all ages. I would like to supply that knowledge when I can. Some people will benefit and others will ignore it. However, it's a part of myself that I am taking the time to share with others. For instance, as a police officer I will come in contact with possibly a million people by the time my career is retired. Let's say 105 of those people I had a chance to save from death and nothing I did worked in their or my favor. There's 10% that I lost. However, there's another 90% that with just a little information, such as giving directions, that I helped. I'm not going to sulk over that 10% that died. Not at all. The position of police officer is viewed negatively because we're never going to be 'crime-free'. We can only do what we can.

We aren't miracle workers. We are going to lose a few cases and people; but, as long as we give it our 'best shot', we did our job. It's hell but that's why you have to enjoy everything about the position in order to accept low pay and high risks."

Robbie said, "I guess what I dislike the most about my position is the nagging of my wife. She'll pick out every negative aspect and shove it down my throat. She doesn't like it because we don't get paid enough for the risks we have to take and she says it's too time-consuming."

I said, "I don't mean to give advice, but if you dislike the nagging so much, tell her exactly what the job offers you and why you continue to perform it."

Robbie asked, "You don't think I've tried that?"

An announcement sounded. "Last call for alcohol!"

I answered, "I'd say that you've tried unsuccessfully and left it at that. However, you're going to have to pick a relaxed moment, look at her sincerely, and explain again, making sure she understands that you're tired of the nagging. Plus, you've got to let her know that you're proud of what you do and why you do it."

Robbie replied, "That's easy for you to say but.

I interrupted, "I've said it myself, to my family that didn't understand why their sister/daughter wanted to be a cop. It isn't an easy task for anyone. Once you figure it all out, sit down with her."

Robbie said, "Thanks for the inspiration. Are you ready to go?"

I replied, "Yes. We have another early day ahead of us."

We exited the club. Outside I put my arm around him to show my understanding. At the car I pulled his body next to mine and said, "I love you and know from experience that you can tell her if you put your mind to it. Don't give up."

Robbie reached around me, unlocked the door and said, "Get in." He walked to the driver's side and together we got into the car. Robbie started the engine, then he paused. He said, "Now I know what's so attractive about you."

Robbie drove the car across the street to room #6. I didn't say anything since I may have said too much. Parked at room #6 I opened the car door and said, "I'm sorry that I'm so understanding. I'm just not the type of woman who stands in the way of a man's dreams. Good night."

I got out of the car and walked to the door of #6. I unlocked it and walked in. From behind I heard Robbie's voice, "Tina, I love you too. See you tomorrow morning. Sleep tight."

I turned and smiled at him as he drove away. I locked the door behind me. I thought how years ago, I had that guy and I really felt sorry for him that he didn't have as understanding of a woman today as he did back then.

I took off the wig and clothes and slid into bed. I thought, tomorrow another death, somewhere out there.

Chapter 11

I awoke at 7:13 feeling very aroused. Lying in bed, I placed hand on my lips. Like a door opening, my lips parted and I surprisingly slid two fingers inside of me. I let my thumb stroke the clitoris as I plunged *my* fingers in and out. I could feel my juices sliding down the crack of my ass. That made me even more excited. At that point, I knew I needed some deeper penetration. I got onto my knees and sat up in bed with my fingers and thumb continuing the motions. I spread my knees as wide as I comfortably could. I quickened the motions of my fingers and thumb. With the other hand, I began to massage my breasts while watching myself in the mirror above the dresser. With each stroke of my fingers I could feel my juices running down the inside of my right thigh. I thought to myself, "Damn, I could use six more inches." To try and bring myself to a climax, I began watching in the mirror my tongue swirl round and round inside of my mouth. The excitement only grew wilder with no climax. After twenty minutes, there was no use. Only more length was going to do the trick. I said aloud, "Damn it!" Still excited I released my fingers from my insides, hopped out of bed to take a cold shower.

In the shower, I turned the nozzle to one direct stream of water. Pointing the nozzle inward the water vibrated my clitoris. The excitement now was reaching unbearable heights. I took the shower nozzle and directed the spray straight up my clitoris. I finally achieved an orgasm but not a 100%. I could really use some physical activity to side-line my thoughts. However with Robbie going to be here soon, I really didn't have the time for anything. I'll just have to ignore my passion for now. I continued my shower trying not to think of anything. I finished showering, got out and dried off. My body was still striving for relief; however, time was too short for me to masturbate again. I grabbed the blow-dryer and dried my hair.

Afterwards, I put my bathrobe on and began combing my wig.

Just then, a knock came at the door. I looked at my watch. It was only 8:15. Oh well. I walked to the door and asked, "Who is it?"

Robbie's voice called, "It's me, Robbie."

I opened the door and said, "You have a bad habit of earliness."

Robbie smiled and said, "And good morning to you, too. Is something wrong?"

I replied, "No; nothing's wrong. I'm sorry. Come in." Robbie walked in. I closed and locked the door out of habit.

Robbie said, "I guess I'm not going anywhere."

I replied, "What?"

Robbie said, "The door; you locked it."

I smiled and said, "Ohhh! It's just a habit."

Robbie said, "You seem a little out of it?"

I commented, "No. This morning just hasn't started off well."

Robbie said, "Well one thing's for sure, you look a lot better as a blonde."

I smiled and replied, "Thanks. I could use the cheering up. Sit down and relax. I have to finish the wig for our outing."

Robbie said, "Okay. I'll give Archie a call and let him know what we're going to do and about when."

I replied, "Fine."

Robbie dialed the telephone and asked, "Officer Sweatbaum, please? Archie, its Robbie. I'm here with Tina now. Well, uhhhh, good question. I know we'll run down to the Bay eventually. Let me let you talk to Tina. Hold on. Tina, come to the phone."

I said, "one minute. Let me get this wig at least ready to put on."

I walked over to the phone which was between the two beds. I took the phone from Robbie's hand. I said, "Thank you. Hello, Archie. Don't let the cheerfulness fool yah. Uhuh, well. Breakfast first; which, since we have to be by a phone will be here." While Archie spoke, I glanced at Robbie. To my surprise, he had taken off his shirt. His muscular, hairy chest made me totally miss what Archie was saying. I bounced back to the conversation, "breakfast and we're negotiating whether to watch a movie or go to the bay." Robbie's hand clutched the end of my bathrobe tie. He pulled the end through the loops of the robe revealing my nude body.

Robbie softly said, "Talk to Archie."

Watching Robbie stand and exit his pants, I said, "Archie, after breakfast if you're not in the office we'll leave a message with dispatch letting you know you can reach us via radio." Robbie disrobed' I felt his hands on my neck, easing downward to the robe, pulling it off my shoulders and down my arms. Continuing I said, "See you when you locate the body." Robbie's lips were kissing my neck as he pressed his penis against my ass. Feeling relief on its way to my aching cunt, I interrupted whatever Archie was saying and said, "We'll wait to hear from you. Good-bye."

I hung the phone up, turned to face Robbie and immediately he placed his lips to mine. His hands began to explore my breasts. Our tongues swirled madly around the other as his hands found their way to my sides.

I found myself not able to resist feeling his penis in my hand. I had waited 12 years just for the moment and I was going to finally fulfill that fantasy. I eased my hand onto his penis. He moaned lightly when I did while we were still exploring the other's mouth. Stroking his penis with pleasure, his hand found its way to my dripping cunt. As we stroked each other, I felt the need to place his penis into my mouth. I interrupted our kiss and allowed my lips to find their way to his neck and down to his chest. Robbie pulled his body away from my lips, picked me off the floor and lied me on the bed. He must have read my mind, for he entered '69' without saying a word. As he parted my thighs, I slid my lips/nice thick 7 inch erect penis-head. He immediately plunged his tongue between my cunt lips. I clutched my hands around the cheeks of his ass, and forced his penis down my throat and back up. He kept his tongue strokes simultaneous with mine. The passion began to roar deep within me. I could feel Robbie's head beginning to expand. Oh, how I wanted to taste his semen. While concentrating on swirling my tongue all around his penis and thrusting it to the back of my throat, Robbie introduced his fingers to my cunt. As he began to tease my clitoris; I started moving my hips rapidly. Robbie followed my lead, and suddenly, he moaned deeply as I received the 'shot of protein' that I had anxiously waited. Then Robbie recovered from his orgasm, he turned his body around to get a direct approach to my cunt. Within minutes of the workings of his tongue and fingers, my body 'shot' straight to the ceiling. Every muscle in me tightened with the release of my orgasm. I lowly moaned while Robbie lapped up my juices. As I lowered my body back to the bed, I said, "thank you. I needed that more than anything."

While still panting as if I'd ran a mile, Robbie kissed his way up to my lips. If there's one thing that we both knew, it was that we enjoyed kissing each other. Nine engaged in a passionate tongue session, I could feel

Robbie's penis reviving against my thigh. With a swift motion, I rolled myself on top of him. Releasing my lips and getting to my knees, I said, "Now, I'll show you why my nickname was changed. From 'TJ' to 'Tex'."

Robbie replied, "I have to warn you, I don't get ridden that often."

Massaging his penis and smiling widely, I placed his penis between my cunt lips and said, "Surprise."

I plunged down hard letting his penis penetrate to its deepest point. I slowly danced circles around his penis until I came back to the head. Once again, I plunged down hard. Then I introduced the 'seesaw' effect to his penis. As I looked into a deep-blue pair of eyes, Robbie interrupted the silence, "You're teasing the hell out of me."

Slowly moving my face downward to his lips, I said, "Yes, yes, yes, yes." Our lips met and the smooth tenderness made me increase the spread of the 'see-saw' effect. Robbie's hands found their way to my breasts. His playfulness only made my passion run wilder.

I pulled away from his lips, placed my feet on the bed and began hopping up and down on his penis. The penetration sent shivers up my spine. I moaned with pleasure. I could see from Robbie's facial expressions that his next climax was going to be soon. I switched from hopping to a quick plunging of his penis. Robbie began to moan loudly.

At that point, I decided that I wanted this 'shot of protein' in my mouth, also. When Robbie began to buck his hips along with his deep moans, I quickly pulled off of his penis and tightly stroked his penis with my hand, while placing my mouth over the head. Within seconds, his warm slightly bitter-tasting semen shot to the back of my throat. I released my hand from his penis and began sucking out any extra.

Then, like a mother cat cleaning her young, with my tongue I cleansed all of my juices from his shaft and balls. Robbie began to run his fingers through my hair as I mothered his penis.

"RRRing-ring," went the telephone.

I pulled my mouth away and began to laugh, and Robbie said, "Shit!" After the third ring I answered, "Hello."

Leaning back on the headboard I smiled widely while Archie said, "Well, we found #4."

I asked, "Whereabouts is it?"

Archie said, "At the north beach right here on base."

I asked, "What?"

Archie said, "Yeah. Get here as soon as you can."

I said, "See you in a few minutes. I know exactly where it i$. Good-bye." I hung up the phone.

Robbie said, "You seem surprised."

I replied, "I am. We don't have to travel too *far*. The body has been found here on base at north beach. Grab a washcloth and get dressed."

Robbie said, "better yet. Let's take the time to hop in the shower. The body isn't going anywhere."

Getting out of bed, I said, "showers not going to come to you."

After a quick playful shower, we dried each other off and got dressed. I bund my hair and slipped on the wig. I didn't bother with make-up since Robbie and I were supposed to be going to the Bay.

Once ready, I grabbed my keys and said, "Let's go."

Robbie jumped into his shoes and followed my lead to the door and out to the car. As we got into the car I was having a hard time trying to erase the smile from my face. Pulling out of the parking lot

Robbie said, "the results of breakfast; I'm tired and you're smiling from ear to ear." We both began to laugh.

I said, "Head down Carter Lane to the beach."

Arriving at the beach, we got out of the car and met with Archie.

I said, "Hi Archie. What's up?"

Archie replied, "Well pretty much the same as the other three, with an exception."

Robbie asked, "Our suspect made a mistake?"

Archie replied, "No, not really. He just encountered a young blonde who didn't want to die. We have some black hair samples that were found on her clothes and in her hand. When we locate our suspect and test his hair, we'll have some concrete evidence to convict him."

I asked, "Anything else?"

Archie replied, "The tram tracks you see have pretty much destroyed anything else."

I summarized, "so we have a profiled suspect who is killing at random; whoever will leave a bar with him."

Archie replied, "Yeah."

I asked, "Any clue as to where she met him or how they got on base?"

Archie pointed to the car windshield at the base sticker and said, "That's how she got on base. According to her ID card, her father is a First Lieutenant. let me show you her face and see if you recognize her."

Robbie and. I both looked at the victim's face when Archie pulled the body bag zipper open. I looked at Robbie and asked, "Does she look familiar to you? I've never seen her before."

Robbie replied, "No. I can't say I've seen her before either."

Archie re-zipped the bag and said, "I hope someone remembers seeing her last night. Well, that's it. Let's go." As we walked back to the car, Archie said, "Otto, call your wife. And you look like hell. Get some sleep."

Robbie replied, "Right away, sir."

As we got into the car, I glanced at my watch. Surprised I said, "It's 12:22."

Starting the car and pulling onto the street Robbie commented, "Don't you know, time flies when you're having fun."

As we drove back to the Inn, I said, "apparently a lot of time." At the Inn I got out of the car and said, "Take Archie's advice, sweetheart. Get some sleep. I had a beautiful outing today. Thank you."

I smiled as he pulled out of the parking lot. He peered out of the window and said, "see you tonight, babe."

I opened the door to room #6, walked in, locked the door behind me, and plopped down on the bed. I thought to myself, he's not just a good kisser; he's a hell of a lay, too. Smiling, I lied back and drifted off to sleep.

I awoke and rolled over onto my stomach to fully wake up. I looked at my watch. "Damn it! It's 5:00." I jumped out of bed. Fluffed the wig and put on my make-up. I couldn't believe, I'd slept that long. I washed and walked to the dresser and pulled out a Polo shirt.

I took the other off, deodorized and put the red Polo shirt on. I looked at the jeans I had on and decided not to change. They looked fine. My teeth definitely needed brushing after not doing so after swallowing two loads of Robbie's come. Afterwards, I said to me, "that's better." I looked at my watch. It was 5:31. Like a detonated time-bomb, a knock came at the door. I walked over and opened it.

Robbie said, "Hi Tina."

Remembering this morning I smiled and said, "Come in. I guess I'm ready to go."

Is I turned to get my purse, Robbie closed the door. Leaning against it, he pulled me by the hand towards him. When our bodies met, his lips found mine. I put my fingers through his hair, showing how much I enjoyed our lips tightly pressed together and our tongues forever exploring the depths of the others mouth. It was a good thing he discontinued because I was ready to re-live the morning.

I said, "It's too bad we have a job to do and no extra time. I'd gladly make-love with you again. However, time's a wasting and we're not getting the job done by standing here."

I turned and retrieved my purse. Walking to the door Robbie stalled. He said, "Before we go, I just want you to know it's going to be hard for me to concentrate on this case knowing damn well how much I want you."

I opened the door and walked out to the car. Looking at Robbie I said, "the feeling is mutual."

Starting the car and driving across the street Robbie parked, looked me and said, "It's not hard to fall for you."

I opened the car door and got out. Robbie did the same, I said, "We fell in-love once. I'm sure it would be very easy to repeat. Especially, since I never stopped loving you."

Bobbie walked to my side. I could tell by the look in his eyes that our lips were going to meet again. However, as he placed his arms around my body, I regrettably placed my hand to his mouth and said, "We have a job to do. Please, try to remember that."

Robbie pulled away and said, "Sometimes you're too damned job-conscious."

I said, "Excuse me! I was told by the General not to let my hair down. That didn't mean from under this wig."

Robbie threw his hands in the air and said, "Fine! We'll do it your way; however, before you leave my side tonight our lips and tongues are going to meet for possibly longer than they have ever before. Prepare yourself. Let's go."

As he began to walk to the clue door I asked, "Are you forgetting that you have a wife and child at home?"

As I caught up with him, Robbie turned to me and said, "No. I'm not forgetting that, what we just said a few minutes ago about love, or what happened this morning. I promise you, I'm not going to forget any of it. Shall we have dinner?"

I replied, "A stiff drink would be more appropriate, however, dinner will do."

Once inside, we did our best to cool down. He was right that I'd asked to be kissed for saying I loved him. However, I couldn't forget that he was married. Robbie showed his ID card and signed me in. We were seated. Robbie ordered two large cokes and the buffet. When the waitress left, our eyes met. I reached for his hand. Cupping my hand over his I looked deep into his eyes and said, "I'm sorry but I'm not sorry."

Robbie rolled his hand over and tightly held mine and said, "I'm sorry for getting angry, too. Nothing more."

I replied, "That's the only apology I'll accept."

We both smiled. The waitress dropped our drinks at the table. "We got up and went to the buffet. Roast beef was the main course.

Robbie commented, "Damn! No oysters."

Embarrassed, with a smile, I turned around, looked at him and became speechless when I saw that broad smile on his face. We made it back to the table without further incidence.

I sat down after him and said, "I can tell now that you're going to remind me of this morning all night."

With a cocky smile on his face, Robbie said, "Enjoy your dinner. Dessert's not far away."

I didn't touch that with a ten foot pole. We ate dinner silently. After dinner, we just relaxed over our sodas.

Robbie broke the silence and said, "Let's go look over the disco and find our usual table."

I said, "Okay."

Robbie grabbed the ticket and paid it on our way out. We walked into the disco separately. After looking around and finding no one who fit our witness or suspect, we met at the bar.

Robbie ordered, "Two oj's please." The bartender complied. Robbie said "you're drink madam."

Handing me the drink I said, "thank you. Shall we exit?"

Robbie said, "Yes, we shall." We walked out to the breezeway and found our usual table and sat down to watch the crowd roll in.

I said, "I'll be damned!"

Robbie asked, "What?"

I said, "Our witness just walked through the door."

Robbie replied, "And so he did. Remember, set a date for tomorrow." As the witness walked to the bar I said, "I'll be right back with your screw-driver. Cover my ass."

Robbie commented, "Gladly and with more pleasure than you'd believe."

As I walked away, I couldn't help but laugh. I walked to the bar and stood beside the witness. I ordered, "an oj and a screw please." The witness turned and gave me a curious look. I looked him up and down and said, "Hello. I'm Tina. Are you alone?"

The witness replied, "Yes but you don't seem to be considering you ordered for two."

I commented, "I came out for a drink with my girlfriend's husband. However, if you'd like, I can make myself available tomorrow night. How's about you?"

The witness smiled and said, "You come straight to the point, don't you? In any case, I have a party to go to tomorrow night for an air-traffic control buddy who's departing the island, would you like to go?"

I replied, "Well, why don't we meet here and after a drink and some communication, it is possible that I'll join you at your buddy's party. I don't have a car, so do you mind driving me there and back?"

The witness replied, "No. That's fine. I'll see you here at about this time tomorrow."

I interrupted, "Well, I'd better get back to my girlfriend's husband." Picking up the drinks and laying a five on the bar, I asked, "By the way, what's your name?"

The witness replied, "Its Joe."

I said, "Well Joe, I'll look forward to seeing you tomorrow night. Bye for now." I walked back to the table and sat with Robbie. I said, "One screw-driver."

Handing the drink to Robbie, he said, "Well, our witness hasn't taken his eyes off you yet."

I commented, "Don't scare him away with that jealous look in your eyes. I told him you were my girlfriend's husband not my lover."

Robbie said, "Well, looks like our witness is having one drink and leaving. I hope you got his name?"

I replied, "Yes I did. It's Joe."

Robbie asked, "Joe what?"

I replied, "You don't get a date by asking for full names, rank and serial number. First names are fine for that purpose."

Robbie asked, "You got the date that fast?"

I replied, "Well, when a woman asks a man for a date, she usually doesn't have much trouble receiving. However, when you guys ask, half the time you receive. It works that way with sex, too."

Robbie asked, "So what time is the date?"

I answered, "About this time tomorrow. Meet here. Then, he has a party to attend. So, once we're away from here and get to the party, you can move in."

Robbie changed the subject and commented, "by the way, you have a nice ass that I want to cover."

I replied, "I see your mind is drifting."

Robbie replied, "With the date set and the witness turned in for the night, how about us following his lead?"

I said, "Since this evening is ending so early, why don't you go home to your wife?"

Robbie said, "I'd rather be with someone who wants to be with me."

I replied, "since we have to meet with the General tomorrow, your suggestion about turning in is a good idea. However, out of respect for your wife, I think you'd better go home. Tomorrow's going to be a long day and we're going to need all the rest we can get in order to be ready for anything. What do you say?"

Robbie replied, "Honestly. Your job ethics suck. You're going to miss what could have been a very pleasurable evening." I was taken aback by his directness. He continued, "However, you're right. We do need to be ready for anything tomorrow. Therefore, I'll go home, call Archie and get some sleep, but not before my lips fulfill their desire."

I said, "Alright."

Robbie said, "Promise me one thing; if you want me afterwards, you'll have me."

Looking into his seductive eyes, I said, "whether I want you or not you're going home to your wife. Let's go."

Walking out to the car, I knew turning him away wasn't going to be easy. Especially, after our lips met.

We climbed into the car and silently drove across the street to the Inn. Not in years had I had butterflies in my stomach like I did at that moment. Once at the Inn, Robbie parked, turned off the motor and slid his body over to mine. His eyes were gleaming with passion which was going to make it more difficult for me just to accept a 'peck on the lips'.

He placed his arms around my waist. I responded immediately by placing my lips against his and running my fingers through his hair. While our tongues played together, I thought how only a fool could not want him. At that point, I made a move I probably shouldn't have made. Being overwhelmed by his gentle-tender kiss, I seated my body on his lap. He responded by kissing me more delicately, slowly bucking his hips and placing his hands on my breasts. Disappointed in myself, I dismounted and pulled away.

I explained, "damn it Here I am doing exactly what I told myself I wouldn't do. And that is seducing a married man." Looking at him I continued, "it's very easy to rekindle a flame that never went out, but it's still not right. You have a wife at home and we need to stop making each other forget that. Please, go home. Please!"

With tears in my eyes, I got out of the car, walked to the door, opened it, and slammed it behind me. Leaning against the door and crying, I heard him start the engine and drive away.

I wasn't as disappointed in myself as I was disappointed that I couldn't have him for my own. Down deep, I hoped he understood. Without turning on the light, I walked to the bed and lied down. Wiping the tears away, I stared blankly at the ceiling and eventually fell asleep.

Like an alarm clock going off, a knock came at the door waking me from a sound sleep. I stumbled to the door, opened it and asked,

"How early are you this time?"

Robbie replied, "Early? It's 9:30. We have to be at the General's office in 30 minutes."

Disgusted I said, "Come in."

I walked to the bathroom sink to wash up. Robbie came in and closed the door. He walked over to me while I was washing my face and said, "You look pretty good in the mornings. Looks like you slept in your clothes?"

I smiled and commented, "Looks like you didn't sleep at all?" Putting on my make-up I asked, "Could you get me a shirt out of the top drawer, please?"

Robbie said, "Sure," as he walked to the drawer, opened it and brought me a white western shirt. He said, "Here you are; can I put it on you?"

Lashing my hands I smiled and commented, "You don't give up, do you?"

Robbie replied, "Sorry madam. I don't know what you mean?"

I turned around and laughed. Looking at his tired face, I took my pull-over shirt off, applied some deodorant and said, "Be my guest."

Robbie smiled with delight, walked over, put my arms through the sleeves and pulled the shirt over my shoulders. Straightening the collar, he proceeded to snap all but the top two snaps. He then asked, "Can I tuck it in, too?"

Smiling along with him, I replied, "As long as you don't stop to play with anything else, sure."

Robbie unzipped my jeans and proceeded to neatly tuck my shirt into the jeans. After tucking, he re-zipped and buttoned the jeans.

I replied, "Very good. Let's go."

Robbie asked, "Uhuh. Can I have a kiss good morning?"

I walked to the door, turned around and said, "Come here."

Robbie walked over. I put my arms around his neck, placed my lips against his and gave him a smooth single tongue swirl kiss and pulled away. Robbie said, "thank you." Reaching for the door knob he said, we can go."

We walked out the door to the car and got in. Is we drove to the General's office, I asked, "you will do a good job of covering my ass tonight, won't you?"

Robbie thought for a few minutes as we pulled into the parking lot. Jumping out of the car, he said, "Let's go."

Mocked, I got out of the car and said, "hold it mister:", as I grabbed his arm and turned him around to face me. He had a shitty grin on his face. Before I could say anything, he Put his arms around my waist and replied, "Always and forever." He concluded with a light 'peck' of his lips to mine.

As we proceeded to walk into the General's office I said, "You bastard."

We both laughed as we approached the secretary. Robbie announced us.

The secretary said, "Yes. They're waiting for you. Go in."

Robbie and I walked in. To my surprise, Archie the General and two P.M.O. members were all present. Robbie closed the door. We both said, "Good morning General, Archie."

Archie said, "good morning."

The General said, "Yes. Sit down. This won't take long." Robbie and I sat down and the General began:

"Tina, you will wear a wire tonight which Officer Otto has possession of at this time. You will be monitored three ways; Detective Sweatbaum, Officer Otto and my two P.M.O. officers. Remember, you're in a mountainous region. If you can, communicate with the subject until you get to your destination. That way, you're back-up will know that the device is working. You will be tailed. However, not too close that the tail will be spotted. That's why I want constant communication between you and the subject. After the subject is taken in for questioning, you're done for the night. Everything will be done faster than it sounds. Try not to be nervous. Relax. You'll have four competent officers covering you. However, always be careful. Any questions?"

I asked, "Sir, if he decides to, let's say, make a stop to get some booze or something, do you want him taken in for questioning from there?"

The General replied, "I think it's better if we stop him after you get to the party. I think it will get less attention."

Archie interrupted, "Otto, you and I will go into the club together and follow Tina and the subject out. P.M.O. will be waiting at the rear gate for us to exit. You'll put the wire on Tina before she leaves the Inn."

I interrupted, "he'll put it on?"

Archie replied, "You picked a hell of a time to turn bashful. The wire has to be checked to make sure it works. So put your bashfulness aside tonight."

Smiling I replied, "Yes sir."

The General said, "One last thing. Don't get lost. You're dismissed."

Robbie and I stood and said, "Good day General." opened the door and walked out of the office. Archie followed behind.

Once in the parking lot Archie said, "5:30 at the club, both of you with the transmitter in place. Tina, do be careful."

Getting into the car I said, "thanks Archie."

Robbie and I drove to the Inn. Robbie said, "Open the door and I'll get the transmitter and bring it inside."

I said, "Okay." I walked to the door, opened it and walked in while Robbie opened the trunk, closed it and followed me closing the door.

I sat on the bed and Robbie asked, "How do you like it?"

Looking at the device I replied, "It looks like a stick-pin. That's going to work in this region?"

Robbie replied, "It did this morning. Besides, if we do lose verbal contact, we'll just have to tail you closer. So don't worry." Robbie put the device on the dresser and said, "I'll be back at 5:00 to help you put it on." He turned and looked at me and asked, "Okay?"

I looked at him and replied, "Do you have to go home?"

Robbie answered, "No."

I slipped out of my shoes, shirt and bra as he walked over to me. Taking him by the hand, I lied down on the bed and said, "I have a pretty comfortable chest that makes a great pillow. If you'd like to accept?"

Robbie slipped out of his shoes, jacket, tie and shirt and laid his body between my legs and his head between my breasts. He wrapped his arms around my shoulders and mine laid a crossed his back, we both fell comfortably to sleep awaiting the 4:30 hour set on my watch.

Chapter 12

At 4:30 the alarm on my wrist sounded. I opened my eyes to find, we were lying in the opposite position of hours ago. I eased myself up Robbie's chest to his mouth. I gently placed my lips against his. Robbie opened his eyes and smiled as I pulled away. I said, "It's time to get ready for work."

Robbie replied, "Let's call in sick and spend the rest of the day in bed."

I sprang out of bed, and said with a smile, "the shower awaits us."

I slipped out of the rest of my clothes, Robbie did the same. We entered the shower together and washed up for our short suspenseful evening. We got out of the shower and dried each other off.

Robbie replied, "It's too bad that we can't call in sick."

Laughing I threw the towel at him and said, "You have a one-track-mind."

I walked out of the bathroom to the sink to fix my wig. I heard Robbie say in the background, "since this afternoon was your idea, I'd say we both do a pretty good job of reading each other's mind."

While brushing my teeth, I just sighed as a comment. We both walked to the center of the room and began to clothe our nude bodies.

Robbie asked, "Do you have another white shirt?"

I replied, "Yes."

Robbie said, "Good. Put it on. That way, I'm sure not to lose you in a crowd."

I said, "Thanks."

After putting my bra on, Robbie said, "wait! Let me attach the transmitter before you put on your shirt."

Robbie walked to the dresser, picked up the transmitter and placed it comfortably between the snaps. He asked, "How does it feel?"

I replied, "I'm not as worried about how it feels as I am about, does it work?"

Robbie said, "Let's finish dressing and I'll test it from the inside of the car while you're in here."

I said, "Okay." We both finished dressing. I walked to the bathroom mirror to put on my make-up.

Robbie said, "After a couple of minutes, say a few words while you're doing that. I'll be right back with the results."

Robbie walked out the door while I began to put my make-up on. After what seemed like a couple of minutes I said, "I'll be glad when I don't have to wear this shit and wig anymore." Finishing my makeup and washing my hands I said, "I know someone who's going to hate it when I leave this island. But, I promise if I'm ever back in town,

I'll drop you a line. By the way, I'm ready for dinner, so get in here."

A moment later, Robbie knocked at the door. He said, "I heard you loud and clear. Let's go."

I said, "I'm all yours." We walked to the car and got in.

Starting the engine, Robbie said, "I'll be glad when you don't have to be made up, too. And yes, I'm going to definitely miss you when you leave, which I hope won't be too soon." We parked the car and got out. Talking to the club Robbie said, "by the way. Anyone ever tell you, you sleep like a baby?"

I replied, "you're pretty cute yourself, especially nude."

We both laughed as we entered the club. Showing his ID card Robbie asked, "Have you seated a Detective Sweatbaum, yet?"

The hostess replied, "Yes. Walk this way, please."

Ve sat down and said, "Hi Archie."

The hostess asked, "May I get you a cocktail?"

Robbie replied, "Two large cokes, please."

Archie said, "Well, I'm glad to see you both so cheerful. Is the merchandise operable?"

Robbie and I both answered, "Yes it is."

Archie replied, "Good. Then we should have no problems. Let's eat just in case Tina's date is early."

Getting up from the table I replied, "I hope he's not as early as the two of you?"

Archie said, "Tina, don't you know that *we* just can't wait to see your beautiful smiling face."

I replied, "Hahahahahah."

Robbie and Archie laughed as we waded through the buffet line. I replied, "Crab again. They must have known I was coming."

Robbie said, "Archie, you should see how much crab this little girl can put away."

Archie replied, "Women from the South are known to get their fill of everything."

I asked, "Everything, Archie?"

Archie replied, "With you? Yes." I laughed as we walked back to the table with our food. Archie suggested, "Let's enjoy our meal and we'll 'chit-chat' afterwards."

Looking at my mouth-watering meal I replied, "I second that." You can bet I enjoyed every last drop. Robbie and Archie seemed to enjoy themselves, too.

After eating, we all relaxed over a cup of coffee. To my surprise, the 'chit-chat' was not over the case. I guess there really was nothing to talk about.

Noticing my silence; train-of-thought, Archie and Robbie placed their hands over mine and assured me, "there's nothing to worry about.

Be right behind you, every step of the way."

Looking at both, I replied, "it's hard to think the opposite when a woman has two good-looking officers backing her up."

As both replied, "thank you", I could feel Robbie's hand grip mine.

Archie said, "If we're lucky, this guy will remember that night and be able to tell us something more than what we already know."

I replied, "That would be nice."

Pulling his hand away, Robbie commented, "If he does know something, why not come to us sooner?"

Archie replied, "We'll cast that stone if the time presents itself."

I said, "Enough! Finish you coffees and let's all sit at the bar. That way, you'll know what I'll know."

Archie replied, "That's a good idea. Why didn't I think of that?"

Robbie said, "drink your coffee, boss."

We finished our coffee. Archie retrieved the check and paid it as we exited the restaurant. I walked to the bar ahead of Archie and Robbie. Luckily there was a couple of vacancies. I sat nearest the door, so I could watch for Joe. Robbie walked up and put his arm around my shoulder. Archie sat down beside me.

Robbie asked, "Can I buy you a drink, Miss?"

I looked at Archie and began laughing to the point that I was not able to answer his question.

Archie answered for me, "order her usual."

After regaining my composure, I said, "The two of you are so tactful."

Robbie ordered, "Three oj's." The bartender complied.

I asked, "Well, what should we drink to?"

Robbie asked, "how about, success?"

Archie and I replied, "Since we can definitely use it, toast."

As we drank, I glanced towards the entrance and said, "I hate to cut this short but our boy just showed." I looked Joe's way, smiled and silently said, "Hi." After showing his ID card, Joe walked over. Robbie shifted his body towards Archie as if they were conversing. I said, "hi Joe."

Joe replied, "Hello. I didn't expect to find you here alone?"

I said, "I stopped in for dinner since they were serving my favorite dish."

Joe asked, "And what is your favorite dish?"

I replied, "Crab and plenty of it. Would you like a drink before we go to your party?"

Joe asked, "What are you having?"

I replied, "Oh! Just an orange juice. I'm a little too full to start boozing."

Joe motioned to the bartender, "Two oj's please." Turning his attention to me Joe said, "I got the feeling from our conversation last night that you were just visiting. Are you?" The bartender brought our drinks and Joe gave him five dollars.

I replied, "Yes. I'm originally from New Orleans and presently reside in Florida."

Joe asked, "I guess you're used to our weather, then?"

I smiled and answered, "Yes. I love the warmth."

Joe said, "We're an hour late for the party. Would you still like to go?"

I replied, "If there's one thing I know about parties, no matter how late you are when you get there, the parties still in full swing. So, why not. Do we have to go far?"

Joe replied, "No. Just five minutes up the road. Are you ready to go?"

I finished my juice and replied, "Definitely. Let's have some fun."

Joe and I walked out to his car. He acted like a perfect gentleman by opening the door and closing it behind me. He walked around to the driver's side, got in and started the engine. We drove quietly up the road to the rear gate.

I began, "so Joe what do you do for the Corps?"

Passing the gate Joe replied, "I'm an Air-traffic Controller."

I played dumb and asked, "Is it a busy job?"

Joe replied, "Most of the time it's boring. But it has its busy days too. I enjoy it."

I commented, "I've heard it's a pretty stressful position. Do you find it that way?"

Joe replied, "Well, it's an area where one mistake can take many lives, but like I said military traffic isn't that popular. Outside the military, it more than likely is highly stressful."

I said, "I guess it's kind of opinionated from one person to another."

Joe replied, "Yes. Just like other jobs. What do you do?"

I paused for a moment and bullshitted, "I have done a lot of odd jobs. I don't really have a career. Just do, to get by."

Joe said, "We have to make a 'pit stop' for a minute. I hope you don't mind? It will only take a couple of minutes."

I replied, "Fine. How far are we from the party?"

Joe replied, "Just up the hill. I only have to get some things from the trunk." Joe pulled to the side of the road just before getting to the house on the hill and said, "I'll be a couple of minutes."

I said, "Okay."

Joe took the keys and got out of the car. I heard him open the trunk. I pretended to be straightening my hair while looking in the rear-view mirror. However, I could see nothing. I sat back in the seat not trying to be nervous. Next thing I heard was the trunk close. I waited for him to re-enter the car and drive the couple hundred yards to the house on the hill where the party was being held.

The car door opened and I glanced to look at Joe. Seeing him, I became speechless. He didn't say anything. I finally found words and said, "You've changed!"

Joe said with a low voice, "Yes."

Ps he entered the car, I heard a click. Looking downward, I saw what appeared to be a shiny blade. I decided not to stick around to find out.

As he moved toward me with the instrument, I grabbed the door handle, opened the door and did a flip out of the door onto the hard pavement. I quickly said into the transmitter, "We have a problem guys. I'm #5." I was praying that my back-up team could hear me.

Once on the ground, I rolled away from the door only to have a 225 pounder land on my chest. With an evil look in his eyes, he raised the knife over his head and came down with it aiming for my throat. With only one chance, I used all the strength I had to quickly move my upper body a foot.

As I did, the knife struck the ground, broke in two and 'rick-a-shade' slicing my ear. As the blade cut my ear I yelled out, "shit!"

Apparently overwhelmed that he was defenseless; Joe got off of me and began to flee. I rolled over and said into the transmitter, "Oh know you don't! You're not getting away': I took off running after Joe and said, "guys, it's a foot race. The house on the hill. Get here now!"

Joe looked behind himself to see me gaining on him. Just then, he crashed through the bay-window of the house.

As I got to the opened doorway, I saw many witnesses standing around. I approached Joe as he dazedly got to his feet. With all the strength I had left, I planted both feet and kicked into his chest which sent him head first into a shelved wall.

Joe slowly fell backwards to the ground. To witnesses and my surprise, his forehead was gashed open.

I looked at one of the witnesses and said, "Call the police and paramedics, please." He immediately complied.

Archie called, "Tina", as he ran through the doorway.

I pulled off the wig since it was irritating my wound. Staring at 4515 and Joe's limp body I sat up and asked, "What took you so long?"

Robbie came through the door and asked, "Are you okay?"

I replied, "I'm alive. But I can't say the same for him."

Archie walked over to Joe's body and checked for his vital signs. Archie said, "he's dead alright."

Robbie put his arms around me and turned me away from the body. To a witness he asked, "Can you get me a wash cloth for her ear?"

The witness replied, "Yes."

Moments later, Robbie said, "thank you", as he applied the warm clothe to my ear.

I guess I was still in shock because I really didn't feel anything. I only knew that I was glad to be alive and held by someone I loved. I could hear the sirens roaring in the background.

One of the P.M.O. officers entered the house giving Robbie my purse and said, "We bagged the broken knife and the 4-T instant tanning lotion for evidence."

Archie replied, "Thanks. Hold on to it. Also, you might put a call into your General. He might want to prepare a statement for the press since this is one of his boys."

The military officer replied, "Yes sir", and picked up the phone and made the call.

Archie said, "Otto. Hold on to that lady. They did one hell of a job. Why didn't we think that this guy could wear a disguise?"

Holding me tightly in his arms Robbie replied, "Maybe, because it's hard to believe that he fooled so many of our witnesses."

The paramedics entered. Archie said, "We need a body bag for him and her ear needs some attention."

The paramedic bandaged both sides of my ear. I could hear the zipper of the body bag. I don't know whether it was harder to believe that the whole thing happened or just that he was dead.

Archie said, "Otto. Take Tina out of here."

I asked, "Archie?"

Archie answered, "Yes Tina."

I said, "I'd like to go back to the mainland."

Archie replied, "I think that can be arranged. Otto, take the lady back to the Hyatt instead of the Inn. I'll pack up her stuff at the Inn and see you at the Hyatt in a few."

Robbie stalled and asked the paramedic, "Do you have something to help the pain?"

The paramedic replied, "Here, give her these. She should fall asleep minutes after."

Robbie and I walked. To the car and got in. I said, "I've crashed a few parties in my life-time but none quite like that."

Robbie replied, "Sounds like you're going to be okay."

I said, "After a shower and a smooth kiss from your soft lips to bring me back to reality, you're probably right."

Starting the engine Robbie replied, "Yeah. You're going to be just fine."

I leaned back against the seat and closed my eyes. I said, "Wake me when we get there."

Stopping the car Robbie said, "We're home."

I opened my eyes and said, "Good." We got out of the car and I unlocked the door. I turned on the light and asked, "Would you like to join me in the shower?"

Robbie replied, "No. I'd better wait for Archie to get here."

I said, "Good idea. Why didn't I think of that?" We both began to laugh.

I undressed and got into the shower. Slowly I brought myself back to reality. You can't get much closer to death than that. I got out of the shower and dried off. I asked, "Did I ruin my white shirt, you insisted that I wear?"

Robbie picked up the shirt and replied, "There's no rips in it, just a little dirty from the pavement and blood from your wound."

Walking over to his side I said, Robbie stood, put his arms around me and placed his lips next to mine. I feverishly accepted his tenderness. My tongue rotated and played like it was the first and last time I would ever kiss anyone again. Robbie pulled away breathless. He said, "I promise. That won't be the last kiss you ever receive."

I said, "You're reading my mind again."

Robbie replied, "No. If I was as close to death as you were tonight, I would have done the same."

I smiled, turned around to the dresser and retrieved a night shirt and underwear.

Robbie said, "I'll get you a glass of water so you can take these pills. I want you to be asleep before I leave. That way, you won't feel alone and fight the medication."

Putting on my clothes I said, "Okay." I walked over to the bed and sat down.

Robbie walked to me with the glass of water and pills in hand and said, "Take them." I complied. Afterwards, I lied back on the pillow and closed my eyes.

Relaxing, I said, "I'm glad to be alive."

Robbie tucked me under the covers and said, "So am I."

A knock came at the door. Robbie opened it and said, "Hi Archie."

Archie asked, "Is she asleep, yet?"

Robbie replied, "She's getting there."

Archie walked next to the bed. Without opening my eyes I said, "Hi Archie."

Archie said, "You did a good job considering none of that was supposed to happen."

I asked, "Will you have a full report tomorrow?"

Archie replied, "By the time I put you on your plane home, you'll know everything. Get some sleep. Robbie, since I know you won't leave, stay with her. I'll make an excuse to your wife if it's necessary. Good night."

Chapter 13

I awoke surprised by a penis sliding between my cunt lips. I moaned lowly as I tried to distinguish fantasy from 'reality'. As the plunging deepened and quickened I said, "So this is what heaven is like."

Just as I made the comment, a body lied on my back placing a pair of smooth wet lips on my neck just below my wounded ear. Feeling my body begin to tingle with pleasure from the motions I commented, "and good morning to you too, Robbie."

His lips and tongue movements quickened with the pace of his thrusts as a response to my comment. I began to moan in delight, for moments away I knew my body would be tossed into frenzy, producing orgasm after orgasm.

Arching my back under his body I cried, "Plunge harder and suck right, there!" Seconds later, my body sprang to life. Rapidly slapping my body against and away from his, Robbie 'shot his load' as a release of one orgasm after another ran through my body until I collapsed from exhaustion.

We lied perfectly still together until both of our cardiovascular systems normalized. I said, "I'll take that any day over an alarm clock."

Robbie pulled his penis from inside of me and said, "I thought you deserved more than just a verbal aloha'." I turned to look at him, instead of saying anything I chose to just smile. Robbie replied, "Now, that's the look I would like to wake up to every morning."

Still smiling, I said, "Ohm."

"RRR-ing!"

I replied, "Archie's awake, too."

Robbie checked. His watch and said, "At 11:00 I'd hope so."

Surprised at the time, I reached over and picked up the receiver. Instead of saying hello, I said, "Hi Archie."

Archie replied, "How'd you know it was me?"

I answered, "Who else would it be."

He asked, "How do you feel?"

I replied, "Oh, pretty relaxed."

He said, "Well, you're going home."

I interrupted so Robbie would know, "My plane leaves at 2:30 tomorrow."

Archie asked, "Here are your bags from the Inn. I had one of my female officer's ensure that we got everything."

I replied, "I can be packed and ready to go in an hour."

Archie said, "I'm seeing the General now. I should be done and very ready for lunch in an hour. So I'll end, the way we began; over a good meal. See you in an hour."

I replied, "Okay, see you then." I hung up the receiver. I said, "Well, we have an hour, give or take a few minutes."

Robbie said, "Now, I'll take you up on your shower offer of last night." Hopping out of bed and extending a hand to me, he asked, "Shall we?"

Taking his hand I said, "Yes."

We both walked arm and arm to the shower. While showering, Robbie said, "Just think. You don't have to put a wig or make-up on."

We both laughed and I commented, "Thank God." We got out of the shower and dried off. I brushed my teeth while Robbie went in the room to dress. I looked at him and said, "It's a shame you have to do that."

Robbie commented, "It's even more of a shame that you do."

I laughed as I reached into the drawer for my last clean pair of jeans and western shirt. Once clothed, Robbie said, "You look good in that color of gray."

Looking at my shirt, I said, "thank you. I like it, too."

Robbie said, "Make sure you pack everything you came with."

Being the 'smart-ass' I can sometimes be, I opened the suitcase and said, "Everything but last night's attire seems to be here." Turning around, with a wondering look on my face, I asked, "What did you do with them? Considering, I went to bed with clothes on and awoke with none."

Robbie walked over to me, put his arms around my waist and said, "Well, the last time I inquired I found that you couldn't get into heaven clothed. Therefore, maybe if you were to look on the floor on the right side of the bed, you might find those evil garments."

I couldn't help but burst with laughter in his arms. I loosened my grip and face to face said, "It's amazing what flows from your lips and tongue."

Pulling me closer Robbie said, "Oh yeah." His lips met mine.

I hesitated, "Make it good. It's the last one."

I placed my lips to his and the passion began to stir in both of us. Our rotations were slow and smooth, one after another. I pulled away to watch my tongue turn around his. Then, I plunged my tongue deep into his mouth. I ran my tongue across his front and back bridge. Afterwards, I returned to the slow tender rotation.

Robbie pulled away and said, "I'm going to miss you."

I said, "I had the memories of yesterday to keep the memory of us alive for all these years and now I have a week's worth to proceed in to the next 20+ years.

Robbie laughed and said, "Yes you do and so do I. Here's your ticket back to the mainland. Are you sure that you don't want me to take you to the airport in the morning?"

I smiled and said," No. I'd rather remember this moment than an airport moment. This is a much better feeling. Let's just say good night instead of good bye. Our paths are sure to cross again.

Robbie said, "That's a deal."

We kissed good night. As he walked out the door, I knew that I had to come back but it wouldn't take 20 years to get back. This Island is way too beautiful for me not to return. I locked the door behind him and headed for the shower. The water felt wonderful beading off my nude body like that of soft fingertips. I felt more satisfied today than I have in a long time.

Chapter 14

After the shower, I dressed in some sweats and walked onto the balcony. I watched as the waves rolled against the shoreline. I felt myself drift back to yesterday when my partners and I would walk and kiss on the beach for hours. You never get to run away from your past. It follows you everywhere. It is nice however to have won two cases and not just one. My pleasant memories of my life definitely out way any of the bad. My adopted phrase of "No Regrets-Only Good Times" is still accurate.

Suddenly, my reminiscence was interrupted with a knock at the door. I walked to the door, looked through the beep hole and opened the door.

A familiar face and voice said, "Hi."

Before he could get any other words out, I interrupted and stated, "I was wondering who I could get to take a moonlight stroll on the beach under the stars. Are you game?"

He replied, "Yes, I'm game."

I grabbed my key and said, "Let's go just like old times."

No words needed to be spoken while walking from room to the shoreline hand in hand. After about a quarter of a mile, I let go of his hand and placed my arm around his waist and my head against his shoulder. He held me close. Then we walked in unity. I broke the silence and said, "Thank you for being you." He replied, "Ditto" as we continued our moonlight stroll.

Just then the alarm clock rang. I awoke and turned the alarm off. I looked around the room to find my Army sweetheart lying next to me in our apartment in Florida.

I couldn't believe that my whole adventure had been a dream. Everything was so vivid and felt so real. Well, at least I can make the most of all the intimate details.

I rolled atop my Army man and enjoyed his willing body parts and demeanor to quench my hunger from my dream state. Oh what a night to remember and a morning for my partner to reap the rewards from.

CPSIA information can be obtained at www.ICGtesting.com
Printed in the USA
LVOW062248140113

315670LV00002B/8/P

9 781479 769001